Watch Your Step: A History of African American Dancing
Volume 1

by
Félix Lambert

Metonym: Information Design

ISBN: 978-1-7381055-0-2

Presented and supported by

((}OUTGANG

Felix is a trusted friend whose integrity and dedication to literature, history and dance is unmatched. He worked tirelessly through his research and writing to bring to light knowledge that otherwise would have stayed dormant and did so without any guarantees that his book would even be published. In an age of misinformation, it is difficult to think of a contribution to society that is more worthy of praise.

Laura Gallagher

In order to properly engage with the African-American dances we love, it is essential to honor the creators by understanding their history and complexity. Our dance community is grateful for this new resource.
Elaine Buchignani

I would like to thank those who supported me in this long adventure: Dominique, for all the love, support, and patience, Félix-Antoine for his passion about music, David, Daniel, Olivier, Ellis, Stéphanie, Xavier, Juan Duran, Rafi, Charlotte, and Warren for their help, and my family for their support. I am also grateful to those who offered precious knowledge and wisdom: Bob Eagle, Lynn Abbott, David Evans, Bruce Bastin, Pete Lowry, Ethan Iova, Hilmar Wensorra, Chris Smith, Ellwood Epps for editing, Greg Gransden for corrections, Heather Ovilla for suggestions, Florence Caron for the design, and all the dedicated people working in the archives. This book would not be possible without the tremendous work of Henry T. Sampson, Bob Eagle, Lynn Abbott, Doug Seroff, Marshall Stearns, Eileen Southern, and many others.

This book exists because of the generous contributions of donors. They are important actors who make this contribution to African American history possible.

Laura Gallager, founder of Outgang
Elaine Buchignani, founder at Swing Dance SCT
Vinith Anand
Anonymous dancer from Montreal
Christine Royer-Artuso
Stephanie Royer-Artuso
Félix-Antoine Hamel, jazz historian at Jazz Viking
Gregory Gransden, dancer and filmmaker
Anne Chevrier, dancer
Daniel Elijah Lévy
Brigitte Dubuc, dancer and owner at Corps En Main; ostéopathie
Paul St-Jean
Brooke Filsinger, dancer and teacher
Mathieu St-Cyr, early organizer of Swing l'Été
Natacha Carrier, dancer
Simon Latraverse, dancer
Liliane Lavoie, dancer
Mélissa Favreau, dancer
Claudia Teucke, VP Commercial Banking West of Montreal
Jean-Marc Limoges, teacher and author of *Victor et Moi*
Lorence Paquette, dancer
Mélina Sanschagrin
Pierre Busnel, dancer
Lucie Dubreucq, dancer
Maria Tzoneva, dancer
Arianne Cardinal, dancer
Diane Talon-Esmieu, dancer
Bonnie Hale, dancer
Aurélie Petit, dancer
Joseph-Marie Tremblay, dancer and organizer at Danses Blues au Parc
David Vachon,
Angelique Koumouzelis, dancer
Natacha Chelly, dancer
Sonia Krol
Typhanie Nolet, dancer
Ola Grignon, dancer
Claire Martinez, dancer and co-owner at Librairie Bertrand
Wesley Loomis
Alexi Morin Duchesne, dancer, DJ, and organizer in the Brussels blues scene
Janine Woods Thoma, dancer, DJ, co-founder and organizer at Green Mountain Blues

Introduction

When I started social dancing almost a decade ago in Montreal, I was not aware this would bring me to my longest research project so far. Like many, I was quickly hooked by the pleasure of dancing and social gatherings, and I took most classes available, traveled for events and workshops and so forth. Quickly, teachers invited me to participate in competitions, but I felt something was missing. My goal was different.

I always loved music and tried to gather a lot of knowledge about it, especially folk music. For instance, I tried to listen and read the liner notes for the whole Ocora collection, which was a challenge by itself. My education also went through music schools as a kid, classical guitar concerts, managing an underground free jazz music venue, and doing university research about the relationship between music and mathematics. Jazz and blues were particularly interesting since they emerged almost simultaneously with recording devices, and it related to my dancing life. It was easy to fall into books on the topic.

After reading more than 100 monographs, I started giving conferences in the community, but quickly realized it only scratched the surface. It led to reading four times more and consulting archives for a book project, and what was supposed to be a book became a book series dedicated mostly to the dance communities.

While writing these books, I avoided certain elements. First, there is no denying that African American dancing takes some of its roots from African dancing traditions. This matter is far too complex for my personal knowledge, however. It would be easy to make general claims in order to give the dances an aura of tribal or folk authenticity, but the reality is that African American came from a wide range of cultural and linguistic groups nurturing their own structures and interconnections to other cultural groups. A dance we like to present as wild and jazzy might find some roots in some prestigious dances; therefore, what we describe as low-down stepping could represent high-class participation and well-refined display in another context.

Also, because of the complexity of the cultural exchanges that occurred, it takes serious work to untangle the genealogy of some steps. In his excellent book *Africa and the Blues*, Gerhard Kubik wrote about the 'blue notes' phenomenon. Kubik's work demonstrates how a lack of serious research on the topic leads to many misinterpretations. Despite the book's first printing in 1999, (more than 20 years ago now), it is common to hear the old stereotypes about the 'blue notes.' Avoiding comparison with African dances in this book is simply a statement that an equivalent of Kubik's work for dances is yet to come, and I cannot pretend to have the proper knowledge to do so.

I avoided making dubious generalizations, which we sometimes hear, like describing African American dances as more sensual. Black society in America was, and still is, multi-layered with different etiquettes depending on place, time, and era. Again, this complexity makes such a description difficult. For instance, to say these dances were more sensual would involve comparisons with other dances of the same time from different cultural groups. The same holds for considering jazz dances, or their music, as rebellious. If such mentions appear, they were directly part of African American interviews, and I rarely discussed the matter within the complex power dynamics internal to African American society.

I tried to keep the writing style simple. I really enjoy historians who are able to add a personal stamp to their books or articles. Still, since there is a lot of material from interviews, articles, and biographies by African Americans, I decided to leave the colorful language to them since the book is a tribute to their culture and not a personal display of my humor or wittiness. My work consists mostly of putting all the information in a specific order, and drawing links that display the rich community involved. Since dancing is related to music, and most historians have gathered material on musicians, it was inevitable to mix dance history with its musical counterparts.

I am aware this book contains a tremendous amount of facts, but these are all the bricks from which knowledge emerges. I have realized over the years that the most important books were often those I needed to read twice, and even more for some sections because the book really had something to teach me, or a change of perspective was necessary on my part to comprehend the importance of some passages.

Sometimes, just knowing the information is available is more useful than forcing an edgy analysis. In writing this book, I intended to create the equivalent of a map of the facts with various paths between them, a map the reader can explore but is not obliged to visit in all its details. For instance, sometimes a list of dancers for specific shows are provided even if some names do not come back later. This is to provide a feeling of the dancing culture's depth and complexity, not just the cold intellectual fact that it was deep and complex. I also believe these dancers would not appreciate being erased from history, as has happened to so many others.

It must be stated that I am not African American, not even American, nor have I lived in the period covered by this book, which will most likely lead to some biases that I hope have a limited impact on my work. This book is simply an attempt to put together pieces of a giant incomplete puzzle. Dealing with writing from the past also implies dealing with unpleasant vocabulary such as the N word and other derogatory terms. I kept them intact in titles and quotes because I believe it helps to understand the difficult context in which African Americans were developing their dance culture and performing arts market. I am aware it might cause discomfort. Some of these words, like 'pickaninny' or 'octoroon' appear in the glossary annexed at the end, to help put their unpleasant meaning in the proper context. Some delicate words concerning other cultural groups are also involved in the body of the text, again in quotes and titles, but are significantly less present.

These first volumes cover roughly the period from 1860 to the early 1920s. Since Marshall Stearns' precious *Jazz Dance* monography, much has been written about jazz artists, blues musicians, dancers and the general African American artistic stage industry. This book is an attempt to bring together, in a comprehensive manner, the dance-related information scattered through all this research, especially the great amount of books published during the last two decades.

The reader will be responsible for the knowledge he or she extracts from the book. As previously stated, it is written in a factual manner and is not primarily aimed at entertaining. Since there is a large amount of information, I wrote the sections so that they point back to previous sections as well as being helpful in understanding future parts. The reader should find her or his own pace, deciding to read more carefully some parts while skimming through others, reading in a particular order depending on personal interests, and so on. It is constructed as a city maquette that the reader decides to navigate. It might not perfectly reflect the reality of the time, but I hope to do my best to reconstruct it as much as possible from the traces left by the past.

In all cases, if the reader craves more details about dance moves, Marshall Stearns' *Jazz Dance*'s annex in Labanotation remains the best source. Nevertheless, as stated by Stearns, one must be careful about excessive precision since dance moves often change from place to place and over time. Even words meaning change over time, as was the case for jazz and blues, and indeed dance terminology.

Readers will not become better technicians by the end of the book, but they might inherit a part of the fantastic heritage left by African American dancers and musicians.

Chapter one: the emergence of an art

Early descriptions of African Americans came through testimonies perceiving them as either grotesque or naturally graceful. Caricature or not, it seems African American music and dance were on the way to charm the world. Noble Sissle, a prominent musician of the Harlem Renaissance, remembered a show in Paris; "It seemed the audience began to sway, dignified French officers began to pat their feet, along with the American General, who, temporarily, had lost his style and grace..(...) Among the crowd listening to that band was an old woman about 60 years of age. To everyone's surprise, all of a sudden she started doing a dance that resembled 'Walking the Dog.' Then I was cured, and satisfied that American music would some day be the world's music." [1]

In her monograph *The Games Black Girls Play: Learning the Ropes from Double-Dutch to Hip-Hop*, Kyra D. Gaunt mentioned her work was an investigation into the epistemology of 'musical blackness,' or "uncovering ways of knowing African American musical aesthetics and musical identifications through an embodied practice." The cultural context started on the ships where "traditional dance was, of course, forbidden on the slavers, but there is evidence that something called 'dancing' occurred in the middle passage." Dr. Thomas Trotter, a surgeon on the Brookes in 1783, revealed, "[a]fter the morning meals came a joyless ceremony called 'dancing the slaves.' Those who were in irons were ordered to stand up and make what motions they could, leaving a passage for such as were out of irons to dance around the deck." Nevertheless, as Hazzard-Gordon pointed out, "[w]e can only speculate about the degree to which the middle passage transformed dance for African slaves." [2-4]

The dances did not disappear on the land where they were sold, and "[s]ome slave masters established 'praise houses' and permitted their enslaved African Americans to 'shout' or engage in secular dancing, even though their peers often disapproved." A small list of dance labels from the plantations include the Buzzard Lope, Wringin,' Twistin,' Breakdown, Pigeon Wing, Cakewalk, Charleston, Set the Flo,' Snake Hips, Pitchin' Hay, Corn Shuckin' and Cuttin' Wheat (the three last as an embellishment of the Cakewalk). It is not surprising to see references to dances done at work or inspired by working conditions proving Gant's point about the importance of the cultural context. [5]

Our goal is to provide a more significant understanding of the African American dances and their contexts for the period of 1860 to 1960.

White observers witnessed some dances during the 19th century. Hentz, for instance, gave an account of the Virginia Breakdown, Georgia Shuffle, Alabama Kick-up, Louisiana Toe-and-Heel, and the Tennessee Double Shuffle in 1854. Some authors have tried to place them in time, like Henry Kmen placing the appearance of the Fandango, Virginia Breakdown, and Jigs by enslaved African Americans before 1837. Black artist Coot Grant, born Leola B. Pettigrew in Birmingham in 1892, named some plantation dances like the Slow Drag, Fanny Bump, Squat, Mooche, Funky Butt, and other classics like Fish Tail, Eagle Rock, Buzzard Lope, and the Itch. Grant became a popular entertainer on the vaudeville circuit between the 1910s and 1930s. [6-8]

Inevitably, some dances bore resemblance to white counterparts, as in 1785, in Virginia: cotillions, minuets, Virginia and Scotch reels. It is hardly surprising since many enslaved African Americans doubled as musicians in rural and urban areas, and some free African American men composed music.

One such man, Francis Johnson, born in Philadelphia in 1792, played the keyed bugle and violin with his orchestra for parades, balls, and dance schools. He composed over 200 pieces, including cotillions, quadrilles, quick-steps, marches, stylized dances, and minstrel songs. Johnson became famous in 1818 when his *Collection of New Cotillons* was published. Some of his titles include the 'Voice Quadrille' (1840) and 'Connor's Five-Step Waltz' (1840). He also composed 'Six Sets of Cotillons' for his military band. On dancing nights, he would change his band name to Johnson's Celebrated Cotillon Band or Johnson's Fine Quadrille Band. His student Aaron J.R. Connor composed an 'American Polka Quadrille' and the 'Philadelphia Hop Waltz.' Similarly, Joseph William Postlewaite penned the 'St-Louis Grey's Quick Step,' 'Dew Drop Schottisch,' 'Lola Waltz,' and 'Galena Waltz.' Johnson also proudly composed a theme on the independence of Haiti. It is difficult to determine what these early African American dances involved in terms of movements. Still, it seems that Johnson's group participated in an early dance craze in the first half of 19th-century Philadelphia. [9]

Images of African Americans also have a long history that helps to establish a cultural context for dancing habits. The painting *The Old Plantation* from the late 18th century is one of the earliest depictions of African American culture. It was discovered in South Carolina and probably came from a plantation near Charleston and Orangeburg. The image shows a male adult dancing with a stick in a half-bent position in front of two women waving handkerchiefs, accompanied by the music of a banjo and a drum. The other early important painting of the time is Samuel Jennings's *Liberty Displaying the Arts and Sciences* from 1792. It presents African Americans dancing and musicians in the background. The following decades left mostly sparse drawings of African American activities, including work, dance, and life in the quarters. Christian Mayr's painting *Kitchen Ball at White Sulphur Springs* of 1838 is an interesting one demonstrating a couple dancing in elegant attire. English naval officer Frederick Marryat recalled attending the evening but noticed a missing musician in the picture. Mayr responded, "I could not put him in; it was impossible; he never plays in tune. Why, if I put him in, Sir, he would spoil the harmony of my whole picture." [10-12]

William Sidney Mount was one of the rare artists who produced many paintings of African American musicians. His *The Bone Player* and *The Banjo Player*, both from 1856, are now famous, but we will focus more on some of his drawings of the dancers.

Religious activities were another common subject of various paintings and drawings of the 19th century depicting enslaved Black people. This would include Russian diplomat Pavel Petrovich Svinin's *Negro Methodists Holding a Meeting in Philadelphia* from 1812, the anonymous *Meeting in the African Church* of 1853, Cincinnati, or some drawings by caricaturist Thomas Nast in 1863. A rather extensive body of music-related images provides insights into African American traditions since their production was made over a few centuries by different artists, but it would be cumbersome to list.

The visual depiction of rural African American dances shares a parallel history. After the previously mentioned watercolor *The Old Plantation* comes *In Ole Virginny*, a wood engraving of 1876 where a banjo player sings, leaning back in a chair,, with two children dancing in the grass, each lifting a leg while their arms seem to be pushing towards the ground. They share similar steps and posture to the dancing child of Edwin Austin Abbey's *Slaves Quarters in the Cellar of the Old Kickerbocker Mansion* published the same year. One couple dances outside to violin music in John Williams Orr's *Negro Quarters*, published in 1853. The men lift an arm and a leg while the couple keeps a distance.[13]

Henry William Ravenel recalled the dancing in South Carolina around the 1830s-40s: "The jig was an African dance and a famous one in old times before refined notions began to prevail... It was strictly a dance for two, one man and one woman, on the floor at a time. It was opened by a gentleman leading out the lady of his choice and presenting her to the musicians. She always carried a handkerchief held at arm's length over her head, which was waved in a graceful motion to and fro as she moved. The step, if it may be so-called, was simply a slow shuffling gait in front of the fiddler, edging along by some unseen exertion of the feet, from one side to the other–sometimes curtsying down and remaining in that posture while the edging motion from one side to the other continued." Ravenel continued, "Whilst this was going on, the man danced behind her, shuffling his arms and legs in artistic style, and his whole soul and body are thrown into the dance. The feet moved about in grotesque manner stamping, slamming, and banging the floor not unlike the pattering of hail on the housetop..." [14]

As explained by Southern and Wright, the dance motifs after 1860 are pretty similar to antebellum times. "The men execute huge leaping steps, assume extravagant body positions and contortions of the limbs, constantly cross the legs, take heel-toe spins, and sometimes flourish a hat in the air." Meanwhile, women usually kept daintier steps. [15]

Christan Schussele's *Negro Village on a Southern Plantation* from 1852 presents the motion of the man waving a hat but in a dance fronting another male dancer. Henry Bibb's *The Sabbath Among Slaves* from 1850 shows a man with a leg up while a woman offers her back and slightly lifts her dress. Henry Louis Stephens's *The Holiday Dance* of 1852 and Nathaniel Orr's *Christmas Eve Frolic* from 1861 present couples facing each other exchanging lively steps to the music of a fiddle and a banjo. *Winter Holidays in the Southern States* from 1858 has a similar outdoor scene, but the man kicks a leg very high while the woman politely lifts her dress a little for a shy step.

Starting in the late 1840s, the term 'jig' slowly disappeared as the general term for African American dance. It was replaced by the more specific Breakdown, Virginia Hoe-Down, Virginny Breakdown, Alabama Kickup, Tennessee Double-Shuffle, Louisiana Toe-and-Heel, Buzzard Lope, Georgia Rattle Snake, Pigeon Wing, and so forth. [16]

Pictorial depictions of dances can only include restricted momentum and intensity, but written testimonials can offer better hints. In 1774, a young Englishman described a Negro ball: "Their dancing is most violent exercise, but so irregular and grotesque, I am not able to describe it." In Richmond during the 1800s "[t]he ball was opened...with a *minuet de la Cour*...Then commenced the reel...Contra dances followed, and sometimes a congo, or a hornpipe; and when 'the music grew fast and furious,' and the most stately of the company had retired, a jig would wind up the evening." [17-18]

Christmas indeed was another important festivity: "On the morning of Christmas, Col. Alston gave orders that as many beeves might be butchered as to supply all with meat, which as a general thing is not allowed them. No less than 21 bullocks fell sacrifices to the festivity. On my first waking, the sound of the serenading violin and drum saluted my ears even in retirement. During almost the whole of the second and 3 afternoons, the portico was crowded with these dancers, who by their countenance reminded me of the ancient nymphs, satyrs and fauns, and the fiddlers and dancers brought Pan and Timotheus freshly to mind. Some of them who were native Africans did not join the dance with the others but, by themselves gave us a specimen of the sports and amusements with which the benighted and uncivilized children of nature, divest themselves, before they became acquainted with the more refined and civilized amusements of life. Clapping their hands was their music and distorting their frames into the most unnatural figures and emitting the most hideous noises is their dancing." [19]

Corn-shucking festivities would also offer an excellent dancing opportunity. These celebrations often brought together various African Americans from different plantations, and music and dance entertained the workers after a hard day of work. Around the piled husks,they danced with women singing "five can't catch me" while the men would 'chase' the woman with the singing "Sally 'round the corn, 'round the corn." [20]

Songs on the plantation also started to include specific dance indications. Thomas W. Talley wrote in *Negro Folk Rhymes* about the Jonah's Band Party he saw as a child, with the singing "setch a kikin' up san'! Jonah's Ban (x2), Raise up' right foot, kick up high, knock dat Mobile Buck in de eye." And the reprise went "stan' up, flat foot, Jump them Bars. Karo back'ards lak a train o'kyars." He notes that Jonah's Band, Mobile Buck, Jump dem Bars, and Karo were specific dance steps.[21]

A few musicians provided the music, often with percussion, violin, banjo, and quills (panpipes), and the music was sometimes frantic. Quill player George Fleming explained, "[b]oy, I sho could blow you out of dar wid a rai of quills. I was de best quill blower dat ever put on in a man's mouth. I could make a man put his fiddle up" and girls "wouldn't look at anybody else when I start blowing de quills." Willie Blackwell stated that enslaved musicians played good enough music to "make dese Cab Calloways of today got to de woods an' hide." [22]

Tourist Charles Lanman witnessed a corn shuck on a large plantation with "the scraping of fiddles and the thumping of banjos having been heard above the clatter of spoons, soup-plates, and gourds, at the various supper tables," and "a new stampede takes place, and the musicians are hurried off to the dancing ground, 'where the Double-Shuffle and Pigeon Wing' order [was] followed by confusion - and in the madness of the dance there [was] no method." [23]

The first serious attempt to study African American songs and dance came from three abolitionists, William Francis Allen, Lucy McKim Garrison, and Charles Pickard Ware. They collected songs on various occasions on Port Royal Island, specifically in the context of the Port Royal Experiment in which African Americans were given lands on coastal islands to see how they could develop by themselves. They also collected music in Charleston, Nashville, Florida, Maryland, Arkansas, Florida, Louisiana, and other places. Their work resulted in the publication of *Slave Songs in America*, a compilation of 136 religious and secular songs. In their introduction, they discuss a religious dance called the Shout, often done in a circle outside the official church. They quote an article explaining, "[s]ometimes they dance silently, sometimes as they shuffle they sing the chorus of the spiritual, and sometimes the song itself is also sung by the dancers. But more frequently a band, composed of some of the best singers and of tired shouters, stand at the side of the room to 'base' the others, singing the body of the song and clapping their hands together or on the knees. Song and dance are alike extremely energetic, and often, when the shout lasts into the middle of the night, the monotonous thud, thud of the feet prevents sleep within half a mile of the praise-house." [24]

They also commented from their own experiences that "[d]ancing in the usual way is regarded with great horror by the people of Port Royal, but they enter with infinite zest into the movements of the 'shout.'" They added that "the shouting step varied with the tune; one could hardly dance with the same spirit to 'Turn, sinner' or 'My body rock 'long fever as to 'Rock o' Jubilee' or 'O Jerusalem, early in

9

de morning.' So far as I can learn, the shouting is confined to the Baptists; and it is, no doubt, to the overwhelming preponderance of this denomination on the Sea Islands that we owe the peculiar richness and originality of the music there." [25]

The authors gave a specific comment to the song 'Early in the Morning,' noting, "This shout is accompanied by the peculiar shuffling dance, except in the chorus, where they walk around in slow time, keeping step to their song." [26]

Another particularity came in the lyrics of the song 'Charleston Gals' collected in Pine Bluff, Arkansas, in which the "Possum cut the pigeon wing," an early reference to the buck-and-wing dances that were a precursor of the tap dance. It is usually described as steps close to the ground, making noise in rhythm, possibly influenced by the clog dances from the British Isles. The Pigeon Wing might have included flapping arms.[27]

For some French songs collected in Louisiana, including 'La Belle Layotte,' 'Rémon,' 'La Aurore Bradaire,' and 'Caroline,' they wrote that these "were sung to a simple dance, a sort of minuet called the Coonjai; the name and the dance are probably both of African origin. When the Coonjai is danced, the music is furnished by an orchestra of singers, the leader of whom—a man selected both for the quality of his voice and for his skill in improvising—sustains the solo part, while the others afford him an opportunity, as they shout in chorus, for inventing some neat verse to compliment some lovely danseuse, or celebrate the deeds of some plantation hero. The dancers themselves never sing, as in the case of the religious 'shout' of the Port Royal negroes; and the usual musical accompaniment, besides that of the singers, is that furnished by a skilful performer on the barrel-head-drum, the jaw-bone and key, or some other rude instrument." Finally, the 'Calinda,' "was a sort of contra-dance, which has now passed entirely out of use." [28]

The Shout was usually restricted to religious occasions, while the buck-and-wing became the leading underlying dance for minstrelsy until the 1910s and 1920s when it evolved into the tap dance, but it did not disappear either. The social Calinda dance, the minuet, and other European-inspired dances still appeared for social events, but they were slowly disappearing.

Dancers at play also appear in Jacques Prat's lithograph depicting Tallahassee, in Florida, from 1842, possibly doing Juba, in John Williams Orr's 1953 *Negro Quarters*, with a couple dancing, or in Wade Whipple's *Evening At the Quarters*, in 1887, doing a round dance. The buck dances and jigs were also standard, with a leg up, often with arms in the air. Such positions, also appearing on some ragtime sheet music, also appeared in the work of Henry Bibb in 1850, Christian Schussele in 1852, Henry Louis Stephens the same year, and Frank Leslie's *Illustrated Weekly* in 1858. The Virginia Hoe-Down in 1855 and the Breakdown in an image of 1861 labeled the same motion. They were all somewhat similar to the 'Dancing for Eels' of 1848.[29]

In New York City, a dancing tradition appeared at the Sainte-Catherine Market. Thomas F. de Voe testified that butchers, merchants, or the general public would hire Black people to dance in exchange for eels. A famous drawing from 1820 entitled 'Dancing For Eels' presented the phenomenon. The dancers appeared in front of a mixed crowd and stepped on a wooden plank called a shingle, a tradition present on the plantations as well. F. de Voe named the dance the Shakedown. 'Dancing for Eels' also became the subject of a colored lithograph by Eliphamet M. and Jas Brown in 1848. Another related drawing dating from around 1885 also exists.[30-32]

The theater piece *New-York As It Is* used the image of the Sainte-Catherine Market for its promotion and offered a rendition of New York's street performances. The play was presented at the Theatre Chanfrau, which was previously named the Chatham Theater.[33]

One of the only dancers to have as much effect as minstrel pioneer Dan Rice and his Jim Crow character was a African American dancer born around 1825 named Master Juba. As expressed by Emery in *Black Dance*: "Apparently Master Juba had produced something new: a blending of Irish and Afro-American dance tied together by rhythm." William Henry Lane, or Master Juba, learned from Uncle Jim Lowe, a dancer performing in Mississippi taverns. He supposedly worked for P.T. Barnum's circus and competed against white dancer John Diamond. (The Barnum Circus welcomed many forgotten singers and dancers over the years, like African American Vivalla Sanford in 1891) Master Juba is probably the same dancer seen in 1842 by Charles Dickens in the New York Five Points district, which he described as doing the "single shuffle, double shuffle, cut and cross-cut; snapping his fingers, rolling his eyes, turning in his knees." In Stephen Johnson's opinion, Master Juba was also able to provide a good rendition of the following dances: The Highland Fling, Sword dance, Lancashire clog, Hornpipe, Minuet, Polka, and others. [34-37]

Dickens's *American Notes* offered a drawing naming him as 'Boz's Juba.' Master Juba was recognized as one of the best dancers of his time and even got the chance to perform in front of British royalty. In that sense, Lane seems to have been the first important figure to reach wide public recognition in the evolving dance containing elements of both African American and British Isles idioms.[38]

The Juba dance, involving extensive use of body parts to make different sounds, was still prevalent in rural areas where performer Tom Fletcher's family practiced it. "Sometimes, with their thoughts going back to their ancestral homes in Africa, there would be a clapping of hands in place of the musical instruments they did not have. The men would slap themselves on the chest, legs or other parts of the body, creating a rhythm similar to that of real African tomtoms or drums. This patting rhythm was called 'Patting Juba,' and it provided rhythm for the dancing. Afterward, everybody rested, enjoying the good things to eat they had brought with them, before returning home to bed in preparation for another day." 'Tallahassee,' a lithograph by Jacques Prat from 1842, showed some patting play.[39]

Another depiction of Juba dancing can be seen in a drawing by Howard Helmick from 1894 entitled 'The Juba Dance' where a child has one leg up and an arm up, possibly preparing to slap his thigh to the music of an old fiddler and the encouragement of a crowd.[40]

Another African American entertainer working with whites around the same time was Thomas Dilward, who was singing, dancing, and playing the violin before the civil war. Billed the Japanese Tommy, or the African Dwarf Tommy, Dilward was born in Brooklyn around 1842, and by 1853 was working with Christy's minstrels as the response to Barnum's star performer General Tom Thumb. After touring with various other minstrel troupes, he continued his career abroad. The minstrel shows, in contrast, were there to stay.[41]

Even if part of the minstrel show's history goes back to Buffalo, New York was the central city that saw this type of entertainment flourish. For instance, Jim Along Josey appeared in 1838 with Ned Harper as part of his *Free Nigger of New York*, with musicians already starting to put the accent on the counter beat.[42]

As a show, the minstrel spectacle was well organized. The first section was important since it finished with the walk around, a dance related to cake walking, as we will see. The second one, the olio, exhibited singers, dancers, vocal quartets, acrobats, contortionists, magicians, impersonators, and ventriloquists –it often integrated new dance steps. The list of dances related to the minstrel shows provided by Emery was vast and varied. It included the Chicken Flutter, Sugar Cane Reel, Congo Coconut dance, Burlesque African Polka, Corn Shucking Jig, Mississippi Fling, Zouave Clog Reel, Smoke House Reel, Union Breakdown, Fling d'Ethiope, Walking Jaw-bone, Dubble Trubble, and Grapevine Twist.[43-45]

Perry Bradford, an essential figure of the blues and jazz scene of the 1910s and 1920s, describes Black minstrelsy as going at least as far back as 1875, and he is not far from the original Black minstrelsy. If a group of seven enslaved African Americans doing minstrelsy existed already in 1855, they were the exception. After the American Civil War with freed African Americans available to hire, a series of more "authentic" Black minstrel troupes bloomed in the South. Early minstrelsy promoted the idea of Black people as inherently lazy musicians, with their authentic music, plantation culture, and so on, but the Black minstrels demonstrated they could be hard-working artists. Abbott and Seroff explained, "Black minstrel companies stole the audience away from the pale imitators, thus opening a pathway of employment for hundreds of musicians, performers, and entrepreneurs." Late in the 1850s, African American troupes appeared in Philadelphia, New York, Ohio, and New Hampshire, and during the 1860s, in San Francisco, St-Louis, Cincinnati, and Detroit.[46-50]

W.H. Lee founded the first all-black troupe in 1865 and it was named the Brooker and Clayton's Georgia Minstrels, led by an African American named Charles Hicks with a cast of 15 ex-slaves from Macon, Georgia. They gained widespread popularity, and many similar minstrel shows followed their path and used similar names. For instance, Sam Hague also started a Georgia Minstrel company which later became Callender's Georgia Minstrel in 1872, and the Haverly Colored Minstrels toured in the 70s and 80s. Another African American entrepreneur, Lew Johnson, formed various troupes that enjoyed continued success zigzagging the midwest. Some of Johnson's companies were the Plantation Minstrels (created in St-Louis in 1878), the Plantation Minstrel Slave Troupe, the Original Jubilee Singers, the Combination, the Black Baby Boy Minstrels, the Refined Colored Minstrels, and the Electric Brass Band (1890).[51-52]

These minstrel troupes provided a flourishing haven for African American entertainers, and many of them would enjoy fame until the early years of the jazz era. One of them, Sam Lucas, was born in Virginia in the 1840s, before moving to Ohio. Apart from touring with his family's minstrel troupe, he showed skill as a singer, guitarist, and song caller for Hamilton's celebrated Colored Quadrille Band. In 1871, he worked as a barber in St-Louis when the Callender's Minstrel troupes noticed him. He later joined a series of minstrel companies like Lew Johnson's Plantation Minstrels (1871–73), the Callender's Georgia Minstrels (1873–74, 1875–76) for which he sang 'Carve Dat Possum' and played some small roles, and the Sprague's Georgia Minstrels (1878–79) with Billy Kersands and James Bland, two other important entertainers of the era. He also took serious acting roles in the 1870s. Sam Lucas shone as writer, composer, and performer in the Hyers Sisters' 1875 play *Out of Bondage*, co-starring with tenor Wallace King, before returning to minstrelsy. He starred again with the Hyers Sisters for *The Underground Railroad*, but, yet again, went back to minstrelsy. In 1878, he landed another serious role in a version of the popular show *Uncle Tom's Cabin*.[53-55]

Sam Lucas was famous for his diamonds and was once asked to join a show for which the inquirer stated, "[b]e sure to tell Sam to bring his diamonds." Lucas later put on his jubilee show with quartet singing, comic sketches, instrumentals, and his previous partners, the Hyers Sisters. For instance, the Colored Ideal Musical Company consisted of Marie Selika, Isabella Miles Taylor, Alice Mink, the Hyers Sisters, Wallace King, Sampson Williams, and J. M. Waddy. Lucas published many commercial spirituals, from which 'Every Day Will be Sunday' was recorded by the Standard Quartet in 1893 and the Zonophone Quartet in 1906. Lucas continued his path in 1880 with a revolutionary staging of *Uncle Tom's Cabin* where African American actors played all the African American characters. Lucas also took part in J.H. Haverly's Coloured Minstrels, a gigantic minstrel show with 20 performers, including the Bohee Brothers, Billy Kersands, James Bland, Wallace King, and others. In the 1880s, he had his own operatic company, with shows including his musical compositions and comic reinterpretations. Published compositions by Lucas included titles like 'Shivering and Shaking Out in the Cold' (1878), a waltz which he might have sung previously with Abe Cox in the Georgia Minstrels, 'De Day I Was Sot Free' with a schottische section for lively dancing, and 'Jeremiah Brown.' One of them, 'The Jolly Dude' (1883), was to have waltz and schottische versions. An observer of the time wrote, "[h]is get-up as the 'Dude' was quite startling, while the motions performed by his lower limbs in that character were a study for a professor of gymnastics, forming quite a show by themselves." [56-60]

Sam Lucas used to do a strutting dance, helped with a cane, and dressed with a gold watch and a giant diamond ring and sang the comical 'I Can Stand for Your Color, but Your Hair Won't Do.' Lucas performed in vaudeville with his second wife, Carrie Melvin Lucas, a violinist, cornetist, and actress. He stayed in business long enough to join shows around the turn of the century like *The Creole Show*, *A Trip to Coontown* (when Shipp left to join Williams and Walker), *Rufus Rastus*, *The Sho-Fly Regiment,* and *Red Moon*. Other achievements worth mentioning are his tour with the Alabama Troubadours in 1901 and his presence in 1905 at the Chicago Pekin Theater singing 'Under the Banana Tree' and 'Won't You Tickle Me?' [61-64]

During these years, critics still enjoyed his solo performances and monologues. He also joined The Frog group, an influential gathering of African American artists, and participated in The Frog Follies of 1913. He took a small role on screen the same year for *Lime Kiln Field Day* with Bert Williams, and in 1914 played a principal role in Williams Robert Daly's long feature film *Uncle Tom's Cabin*, a script he knew well already. An article about him from Indianapolis recalled his compositions 'Carve That Possum' and 'Every Day Will Be Sunday,' before a final complimentary comment: "He could write songs and sing them, he could dance. He could wear the funniest clothes on the stage." [65-67]

As a child, performer Tom Fletcher remembered that his father always compared him with Lucas, his father's hero: "There was never a home talent show, concert, festival or anything happening in town that didn't have me on tap, singing" and when his father saw him practicing his steps in the backyard, he laughed and told him he would never be as good as Sam Lucas. Lucas, though, was not the only big star of his time.[68]

Billy Kersands was born in Baton Rouge, Louisiana, in 1842 and seemed predestined to a life in entertainment. Sam Lucas wrote about Kersands at his death: "I often sit and think of the funny stories he used to tell me of himself and the old folks at home when he was a boy. Among them, one of his duties was to fill and light his grandmother's pipe, which task had to be performed many times a day. Billy, by way of diversion and occasion, placed a little charge of gunpowder in the bowl of the pipe, piled the tobacco upon it, lighted it and passed it to his grandmother. The mild explosion which ensued gave her a great shock and him amusement." [69]

Kersands had the chance to tour with Sam Lucas in the Callendar's Georgia Minstrels, where Kersands sang 'John's Gone Down on the Island.' Van Eyk wrote in 1913 about Kersands' early years: "He commenced to make people forget trouble and care when he was about fifteen as a shining light of Callender's Georgia Minstrels. His next engagement was with Haverly's Minstrels, the proprietor of which 'discovered' the possibilities of the bright comedian. In his early days with Haverly's Minstrels, Mr. Kersands was a general utility boy. Had not the principal star of this organization fallen ill, Mr. Kersands might have still been washing dishes. The manager had to look for someone to fill the breach. Everyone was selected in turn, but of no avail. There was no one in the company capable of following in the star's wake. When it was time for the curtain to go up the proprietor was desperate. He had to take a chance, so took it with this young Billy Kersands. 'I put him on as a joke,' he told a pressman afterward, 'but it happened to be a mighty good joke. Kersands paralyzed that audience. As for the other members of the company, why, I guess he made 'em look like a pack of amateurs—and they were high salaried people too.'" Kersands recalled the good treatment he received while touring in England; "they treated me so well that I did not know I was a colored man until I looked in a glass." [70-71]

Writer and poet James Weldon Johnson recalled that "Billy Kersands, the most famous of all the genuine Negro minstrels," introduced the Virginia Essence, "which constituted of the fundamental steps in Negro dancing." Sam Lucas added more details about this: "His main specialty was his dance, 'The Essence of Old Virginia.' In that dance, he would lie flat on his stomach and beat first his head and then his toes against the stage to keep time with the orchestra. He would look at his feet to see how they were keeping time, and then looking out at the audience he would say, 'Ain't this nice? I get seventy-five dollars a week for doing this!'" [72-73]

Ragtime composer Arthur Marshall said, "Kersands did the Virginia Essence perfectly." His talent at the Virginia Essence made the Queen of England laugh heartily. Van Eck recalled him saying in 1913, "[o]ne of the most genuinely funny things that have occurred in my career, happened in London, when we were showing at Her Majesty's Theatre. I was executing my Essence of Virginia dance—a combination of knee work and head buttoning to keep time with the music—when all of a sudden the audience commenced to laugh some. My, I thought to myself, I am going some this evening. As laughing grew in volume, the harder I worked. Said to myself, 'Billy Kersands, you are making a sure hit tonight.' Suddenly I chanced to look around to get the shock of my life. There on the stage behind me, mimicking every action and grimace, was a three-year-old 'pic.' Well, I was more astonished than angry and just had to laugh. This pleased the audience so much that they threw money down on the stage in handfuls. Was I pleased? Why, yes, I never knew there was so much money in the world—for that 'pic' got every cent that evening and many nights after, as her stunt went so big that they introduced it as part of my act." [74-75]

Tom Fletcher was himself a minstrel performer. He recalled his early days in minstrelsy. "My place in the first part was just like the boy in the Al. G. Fields Minstrel. The first part was the regular semi-circle, the Interlocutor slightly elevated in the center with five men (three singers and two end men) on each side. The banjo and guitar were just a little behind the Interlocutor. My chair, made especially for me, resembled that today called a love seat, putting me in a reclining position. Nat Lucas was the Interlocutor. End men, Tambos, were Bill Reid and Tom Gales; Bones, Henry Derring, and Frank Green. In addition, the Bayou Quartet and Frank and Willie Jackson, dancers, were also featured." The show lasted a little longer than an hour and a half. The hardship of segregation compelled the troupe to sleep in rail stations and halls in winter. [76]

Fletcher wrote about the great minstrel man, "Billy Kersands was a natural born comic. Large of stature and with an extra large mouth–which he used to advantage in his comical antics–he was also a good acrobat and tumbler and an excellent dancer. His original dance creations were the soft shoe and buck-and-wing, the dances that were very popular in the early days of show business; the type which are still used today in all musical shows, on stage, screen and in television. Now taught by dancing teachers and known as the soft shoe." About this Virginia Essence, "[h]e danced it to a slow, four-four rhythm, and for all of his two hundred pounds, was as light on his feet as a person half his size. The tune he danced to most of the time was Stephen Foster's 'Swanee River.' Foster and Bland supplied most of the tunes of that period. Today, there are hundreds of tunes used for the same dance." Pianist Lovie Austin recalled Kersands was a "very, very funny man," while dancer Willie Covan recalled him singing 'Wait Till the Clouds Roll By.' [77]

The Virginia Essence sometimes appears in the list of plantation dances, and different versions probably existed. Some probably were closer to a mix of buck dance, Soft Shoe, and eccentric dancing.

Indeed, while African American stage performances evolved on the minstrel stage, some African Americans frowned upon it for its vulgarity or the stereotypes it perpetuated. Other institutions quickly got involved in the field, providing a more "refined and respectful" stage presence for its race. Three prominent universities would be essential in promoting African American folk songs during that era. The Fisk University from 1866, the Hampton Institute from 1868, and the Tuskegee Institute from 1881, all of them promoting their touring spiritual singers.[78]

The first to appear was the Fisk Jubilee Singers, created in the hope of raising money for the institution, which, incidentally, was a success. Early during the troupe's career, they sang songs collected or written by others, such as those from Abby Hutchinson's *Camp Meeting Songs of the Florida Freemen*, published in 1870. Working for the institution, Adam Spence addressed the question of the fear of economic viability and the touring students being compared to the minstrel shows. Indeed, in the beginning, they were sometimes described as a minstrel band which also meant a singing group. Even their singing met the need for 'wild,' 'delicious,' 'grotesque,' and 'heart music.' The complexity of their songs was significant as Sandra Jean Graham wrote about the swing, syncopation, and asymmetrical passages while also keeping the material adapted to concert singing. Also, it took the students out of class, and as a result, only one of the original Fisk students finished his degree. Another similar troupe was the Canaan Jubilee Singers, already active in 1872 and raising money for their cause.[79]

The Hampton singers started touring in 1873, and the public feared they were not Christian enough; this issue was soon resolved. Their institute represented a more manual education and training. Therefore, the public considered them less cultivated and cultured, but in the end, they gave performances seemingly more characteristic of 'slave songs.' A critic in New York even talked about the 'shout leader' Joseph Towe, uplifting both the singers and the audience. Their performances focused more on the folk tradition than the Fisk Singers. In the same perspective, there were the Tennesseans, also claiming to sing folk-rooted spirituals and calling their shows "slave cabin concerts." They also integrated a shouter. The Wilmington Jubilee singers, starting in 1874, were closer to the Fisk singers in style while adding Southern scenes like the Tennessee singers. They added bone players, comic dialogues, and so on. For these troupes, it is unclear if they actively performed the shout dance on stage.[80-83]

As discussed by Graham, the popularity of these spiritual performing troupes led to the current of 'commercial spirituals' at the end of the same decade. Graham named over 40 touring jubilee troupes active between the Fisk innovation and 1881, some of them using the term Troubadours, like the Hopkins Colored Troubadours, and Troubadour Negro Quartette. All of these influenced the minstrel shows; some minstrels even scheduled their shows as camp meeting sideshows.[84-85]

One representative troupe in this tradition was the Hyers Sisters company. The sisters, Anna Madah, born in 1855, and Emma Louise, born in 1857, started performing in the 1860s. They teamed up with tenor Wallace King, John, and Alexander Luca from the Luca Family, and formed the Grand Colored Operatic Concert Troupe. At first, they sang secular songs, but they added spirituals to suit the market and finally fully embraced them. Pauline Elizabeth Hopkins, born in 1859, wrote articles and plays and sang with her parents in the Hopkins Colored Troubadours. In 1879, she wrote *Peculiar Sam, or The Underground Railroad*, to promote Sam Lucas. She shortened and renamed the play *The Slave's Escape, or, The Underground Railroad*. It was similar to *Out of Bondage* in some parts, like Sam Lucas's burlesque sermon. The Hyers Sisters performed it, but difficulties arose with the show when Lucas left the troupe.[86-88]

As demonstrated by Graham, the minstrel tradition was close to spiritual music, with some leading performers writing songs fitting both the secular and spiritual categories. For instance, Sam Lucas' 'Golden Raft' flirted with the religious, and 'Carve Dat Possum' from 1875 was inspired by 'Go Down Moses,' a freedom hymn popularized by the end of the American Civil War. In 1881, Lucas composed at least 21 spirituals and started his Ideal Jubilee Singers, including the Hyers Sisters, a violin solo, and other attractions. He presented spirituals consistently in the jubilee context, contrary to minstrel shows, a market he tried many times to escape. Also crossing that line, Jacob Sawyer, who wrote 'Out of Bondage Waltz' for the Hyers Sisters, was a pianist who wrote mazurkas, marches, polkas, schottisches, and spirituals. James Bland's 'Golden Slippers' also entered that category.[89-92]

The crossover of such songs from spiritual to minstrel stages sometimes shocked audiences. Robert Moton, who succeeded Booker T. Washington as president of the Tuskegee Institute in 1915, wrote about his early days in Virginia around 1878. He remembered attending a circus show with blackface comedians in a semi-circle playing banjo and tambourines, explaining "how shocked I was when they sang, 'Wear dem Goden Slippers to Walk dem Golden Streets,' two men dancing to the tune exactly as it was sung by the people in the Negro churches of my community."[93] In the same trend, Pete Devonear, who composed the 'first' commercial spiritual, 'Dar's a Meeting Here Tonight,' was an endman playing tambourine and banjo in the Georgia Minstrels between 1871 and around 1884. He also published the standard 'Keep 'a Movin" in 1885. 'Dar's a Meeting Here Tonight' was the most popular of Devonear's five credited compositions and a national hit. During the late 1870s and later, the terms shout, plantation songs, slave hymns, and chants were often equivalent in the press. The classic 'Old Black Joe' is another standard from the same era.[94-95] In addition to the traditional spirituals, minstrel shows offered many jubilee parody songs like 'Carry the News! We're All Surrounded,' 'Rock' a My Soul,' and 'Contraband Children,' all from the early 1870s. For instance, Charles Hicks's Georgia Minstrel helped popularize 'Carry the News.' 'Rock' a My Soul' even found a place in the landmark compilation *Slave Songs of the United States*. 'Contraband Children' was first conceived as a dance number, just like 'Carry the News to Mary.' Finally, the decade saw the emergence of what Graham called commercial spirituals like James Bland and Mannie Fried's 'In the Evening by the Moonlight' from 1881. Even social dancing was sometimes related to religious performances, as in Baltimore, where a picnic dance organizer hired a band in 1891 for a popular camp meeting, or the Old Jubilee Singers' concert, in Pittsburg, after which a social dance occurred.[96-101]

The main troupe to emerge and include secular and spiritual songs in that decade was The Original Nashville Students. Formed in 1882 in Chicago, the non-school related cast of eight or nine members presented spirituals and plantation scenes, a quartet, and finished with a small sketch. They sang Sam Lucas's 'Every Sunday Will Be Sunday' and similar titles.[102]

The term 'coon' also became increasingly popular in music titles, showing a strong continuity with the minstrel tradition. For instance, James Putnam wrote both spirituals and songs with 'coon' in the title and Sam Lucas published 'De Coon Dat Had de Razor' in 1885. Despite the self-parody of 'coon songs,' African American composers continued to include social statements. Jim Grace, another active composer in the 1880s, penned 'All de Darkies Gettin' Up,' incorporating the critique of white behavior; "He prays so loud on Sunday, he whips us all on Monday." This line echoed in songs for the next 50 years at least.[103-104]

Some concerns about religious practices, though, would also come from within the community. Daniel Alexander Payne, born 1811, and bishop for the African Methodist Episcopal Church, saw a ring shout in 1878 and described it in pejorative terms using epithets like 'stupid,' 'extravagant,' and 'disgraceful.' During these decades, the shout received some hostile criticisms from prominent African American religious personalities who considered this tradition primitive and heretic. The Shout, being well-rooted already, survived in many areas, both in rural and urban contexts.[105]

If northern cities like Philadelphia, New York, Chicago, and St-Louis held a vital role in the evolution of African American culture, the South also had significant cultural centers like Charlestown, Birmingham, Atlanta, and, indeed, New Orleans. The dancing in this city appeared as naturally as the Louisiana governor William Claiborne summed it up: "The story of music in New Orleans must begin with dancing." [106]

The main path for African enslaved people to the United States passed through the Caribbean, where their sojourns put them in contact with dances from other captives and locals mixed with a European heritage. The main dances were the Calinda, Chica, Bamboula, and Juba. The Calinda was seen in the West Indies as early as 1798, but there was also a cajun dance called Colinda. They all included the main elements common to the analysis of African American dances: polyrhythms, asymmetry, torso and hip isolations, and so forth. Sometimes these would be staged in a circle of dancers, while some soloists would perform in the middle. Some traditions included partner-oriented dancing as described by F.W. Wudermann in Cuba in 1844: "Presently woman advances and commencing a slow dance, made up of shuffling of the feet and various contortions of the body; thus challenges a rival from among the man." [107-111]

In Cuba, some steps would emerge from the French contredanse, producing the contradanza habanera. Cuban music would also mix in Mexico with a population that would later move to the New Orleans French Quarter. 80% of the enslaved people in the United States came through the Caribbean, mainly around the 18th century; the owners usually relocated them to Virginia, Georgia, and the Carolinas. As a principal important observation, Emery concluded from her lengthy study that "[s]ince so many of the Africans imported to the United States were from the West Indies, and since many of the mainland slaves were seasoned in the West Indies, it is highly probable that the dances reached the mainland." The independence of Saint-Domingue (Haiti) in 1804 also brought as many as 10 000 immigrants within a decade. [112-116]

In Berry's words about New Orleans, "[n]o other American city has such a pronounced African identity." Because of the creoles from Haiti, there were free Black people in the Crescent City. Being 'black' did not necessarily mean being a slave, nor did being white mean having power, as was the case with the populous Irish and Italian communities. The city proved a rich environment for cultural exchanges. Some essential names in jazz history had a rich genealogy, like Louis and Lorenzo Tio. Born in Mexico of African, French, and Choctaw descent, they taught a whole generation of jazz musicians. For his part, Manuel Manetta was an Afro-Italian creole. [117-119]

There used to be many locations for enslaved people to celebrate their culture in the city, like on the Levee and at Lake Pontchartrain. John Watson saw African Americans on the levee performing songs and dances, and Christain Schultz, four years later, in 1804, saw 20 different dancing groups with leaders dressed in a wild fashion. In 1817, the law restricted dances to Congo Square. [120-121]

Some dancers were probably practicing some mixture of various religious dances, including Voodoo (sometimes used as a general word for 'black' practices of African origins). Still, Emery states that the dances practiced publicly at Congo Square would most likely not be sacred Voodoo dances. This is because it was a public space controlled by whites, so religious practices probably existed in secret locations, like mambo Marie Laveau's celebrations by Lake Pontchartrain on a piece of land she owned. The dances evoked in Congo square are the Bamboula, the Calinda, the Chacta, the Coonjine, the Congo, and similar Afro-Caribbean dances.[122-124]

Moreau de Saint-Mery described the Bamboula seen in the Caribbean and Louisiana: "The group forms a kind of chorus, replying to one or two principal singers whose remarkable voices repeat or improvise in a song. A dancer and his partner, or a number of pairs of dancers, advance to the center and begin to dance, always as couples" with women hand-clapping on the sides. Another precise testimony came from the hand of Henry Didimus, who witnessed the Bamboula at the square. "The head rests upon the breast or is thrown back upon the shoulders, the eyes closed, or glaring, while the arms, amid cries, and shouts, and sharp ejaculations, float upon the air, or keep time, with the hands patting upon the thighs, to a music which is seemingly eternal." Didimus added, "[t]he feet scarce wider than their own length; but rise and fall, turn in and out, touch first the heel and then the toe, rapidly and more rapidly, till they twinkle to the eye, which finds its sight too slow a follower of their movements." [125-127]

George Washington Cable mentioned the quills and dancing to "Quand patate la cuite na val." He wrote, "[t]he bamboula still roars, and rattles, twangs, contorts, and tumbles" and "the music changes. The rhythm stretches out heathenish and raged. The quick contagion is caught by…the crowd, who take it up spirited smitings of the bare sole upon the ground, and of open hands upon the thighs." Rudi Blesh called these dances Counjaille or Coonjine rag dance, whereas African Ameircan blind composer Louis Moreau Gottschalk composed a 'Bamboula' inspired by similar scenes in Congo Square. While it is probable that African Americans did a wide variety of dances in Congo Square, it is difficult to be sure of the distinctions from the Caribbean dances since the same general principles of body movements were involved. Concerning the music, it is clear that multiple instruments were used, including various drums, string and wind instruments.[128-131]

Working from oral testimonies, Edward Kemble drew celebrations at the Square around the late 18th century for an article by Latrobe, who described the dancing as slow and dull. Nevertheless, "shortly after 1835, the Congo Square dances ceased." While the authorities banned some celebrations starting in the 1840s, the activity in the public space never entirely disappeared. In the 1890s, Creole brass bands were rehearsing in the area.[132-133]

For Robert Goffin, traditions at Congo Square mixed with French musical heritage and evolved into ragtime between 1800 and 1900. Henry Kmen perceived Congo Square as the synthesis between Afro-Cuban-Haitian immigrants, French creoles, and anglos, which became the source of songs like 'Jim Along Josey,' 'Yellow Gals,' or 'Old Virginia Never Tire.' The city's geographic situation led some of these to the shanties' repertoire.[134-135]

There is likely a link between the music heard at Congo Square at the time and the jazz to come, but without direct records, it is risky to assert. In any case, Congo square was a primordial cultural center for the living generations preceding the ragtime, blues, and jazz musicians from New Orleans and, as a result, for the dancers. In his autobiography, Sidney Bechet rooted his musical abilities precisely at Congo Square, where his grandparents met when his grandfather played drums. It is also where his father, a reputed dancer of the Square, charmed his mother.[136-137]

Another local particularity was the quadroon ball. The situation with these balls was complex. Black people and white patrons often attended the same ballrooms but for events held on different days. It led to complaints about African American evenings imitating white luxury. The argument made by a man named Barran to the city council was that African Americans could only afford this luxury by stealing. As a result, the board restricted colored ball dances to private homes in the early 1800s. Some official documents provided details about these activities. The report of a police raid at a private African American ball described the settings with one room for the cotillion and the other for the Virginia Breakdown with a small orchestra.[138-139]

In response to the ban, businessmen Coquet and Boniquet started to have exclusive colored dances on Sundays at their theater. Still, smaller venues and less respectable places also held dances. In 1805, Auguste Tessier organized a weekly dance for free women of color at the Tivoli in Bayou St-John, dances from which colored men were excluded. Later Coquet also promoted quadroon balls. In 1808, the Union Ballroom on Ursuline Street offered its first quadroon ball, and from then on, many followed. For Kmen, the quadroon balls drew many white patrons and became places for prostitution and 'placement.' Murders and duels became a common sight. White women started to go masked at balls to survey men's activities even if attending was prohibited. quadroon balls remain a delicate topic since they underlined power dynamics between African Americans and Caucasians in the city, as well as those between Creoles and Black people.[140-142]

Mix marriages led to a long list of distinctions for various degrees of creolization, from quadroons to octoroons and even more. For Hazard-Gordon, it was organized exploitation of black bodies with tickets to attend, a 'plaçage' system for white men to find exotic concubines. Bernardo Coquet and José Boniquet's transformation of their theater into a quadroon ball demonstrates it was a lucrative business. As Hazzard-Gordon puts it: "These functions were essentially glorified slave marts. Mothers brought their thirteen- and fourteen-year-old daughters, dressed in their finery, and paraded them for inspection. Surveying a group of quadroon girls, the 'patron' was virtually assured of the young women's virginity." White patrons also danced with the prospects they were interested in pursuing.[143-145]

Focusing only on Congo Square and balls, though, would overshadow other sources for entertainment like John 'Picayune' Butler, a street musician and Juba dancer who found residence at the St-Charles Theater in the 1830s and was immortalized in the song 'Picayune Butler's Come to Town.' He would have taught blackface comedian George Nichols to sing and dance Jump Jim Crow. Nichols was known to have popularized the dance-inspired minstrel song 'Claire de Kitchen' after hearing it sung by firemen on the Mississippi River. Another influential street musician was Old Corn Meal, a singing and dancing New Orleans street vendor from the same decades who also played at the St-Charles Theater. Old Corn Meal was also at the Camp Street Theater in 1840.[146]

There were some early recordings done in the city by the Louisiana Phonograph Company, including some by Louis 'Bebe' Vasnier, a creole born in 1858 who was a comic actor and banjo player. He took part in the Johnson and Vasniers' Colored Minstrels in the 1880s and, finally, recorded in 1891 as Brudder Rasmus, including 'Adam and Eve and the Winter Apple.' Vasnier later relocated to St-Louis, where he was known for his comical monologues.

For pioneering recordings outside New Orleans, we have to look mainly for harmonizing barbershop quartets. By the 1900s, barbershop ensembles were so widely spread that you could barely find an African American man not belonging to one. Their appearance on record started with the Unique Quartette, which Edison recorded in 1890. They sang titles like 'Mamy's Black Baby Boy,' 'I'se Gwine Back to Dixie' and 'Who Broke the Lock,' a theme that reappeared in some blues, jazz, and hokum songs. The following year, it was Colombia's turn to take a chance on barbershop music, with the Standard Quartette and songs like Pete Devonear's 'Keep Movin.'' Then came the Dinwiddie Colored Quartette with 'Down on the Old Camp Ground,' and 'Poor Mourner,' a song already recorded by the Standard Quartette and the first recorded song by bluesman Frank Stokes as 'You Shall' a few decades later. The song also contained a recurrent phrase found in blues with "girl working in the white folk yard." The other recording quartets in the subsequent years were the Apollo Male Quartette and the curious Polk Miller and His Old South Quartette. Miller was a businessman centered on African American music who hired a quartet to back his banjo playing. Quartets like those who recorded were part of both social contexts and the minstrels and religious traveling shows.[147-148]

Back in New Orleans, the years after Vasnier's first recordings would be the starting point of an important string and brass band tradition. Examples were the Tio String Band, Nickerson's String Band, and the Doublet String Band hired for a dance festival in 1889, with musicians like Charles Doublet, William J. Nickerson, Lorenzo Tio, Paul Dominguez, and others.[149]

An iconic one was the Buddy Bolden Band. Bolden was born in 1877. He learned the barber trade and played the cornet. His band, active between 1895 and 1906, was the most significant early ragtime and jazz band in New Orleans. These bands bloomed everywhere.

The 1890s saw the emergence of musical genres widely associated with African Americans. Although a precise portrait of the music of the time is impossible to sketch, the overall perspective suffices. We know that military bands were a common path to musical training and that fiddles and banjos were quite popular. Brass and fiddle bands were probably prominent in rural and urban communities and were influential in mixing African American and Caucasian dancing practices, as demonstrated by Smith in his analysis of William Sidney Mount's paintings and drawings. Perry Bradford mentioned the Lambert Family Band formed in 1867 in New Orleans with a vocalist, tuba, bass violin, and harp, which changed its name in 1872 to the St. Bernard's Brass Band. The decreasing prices of guitars also made the instrument a new favorite. Some musicians trace back the blues from around this time; Big Bill Broonzy thinks 'Joe Turner Blues' is from around that time, and other blues references came from the turn of the century. Handy mentioned songs from that era like 'Joe Turner,' 'Careless Love' or 'Stagolee' were not labeled yet, "we didn't call them blues in those days." [150]

Inevitably, new dances accompanied the emerging music, and some disapproved. In 1895, an article appeared around the eternal debate about dancing being better in the old time. A new generation of dancers brought various steps, different from the previous ones that included square dance callers like Sam Lucas and buck and wing specialists. Praising the older generation, the article indicated that "[w]hen they danced, they displayed an agility with their feet, that resembled the wings of a human bird and double shuffled and cut 'the pigeon wing' in a manner that the young generation can no more do than they can fly." The article complimented a specific fiddler and caller: "As for Si Williams, he could literally make his fiddle talk. He could ask the dancers by his fiddle 'to draw partners,' and then he could ask, 'if they were ready,' and finally, when they had danced sufficiently, he could say with his fiddle, 'you had better rest awhile.'" [151]

The main African American musical style to reach wide popularity at that time was ragtime. Pianists like Scott Joplin were already practicing the style in various locations. Still, the presence of ragtime pianists, including Joplin, on the periphery of the Chicago World's Fair of 1893, propelled the music to the front of the scene.

A loose definition of ragtime would be a syncopation of classical music, marches, quadrilles, and popular music of the time. By extension, it also includes compositions expressly made in that style. Pianist and composer Eubie Blake defined ragtime in these terms: "Ragtime is syncopation and improvisation and accents." [152]

Eileen Southern suggested that Francis Johnson was already improvising on his quadrilles in the 1830s. As she conjectured, there was probably a conception of hot music before the word ragtime was conceived, for instance, in the Five Points area of New York, already known from 'Dancing For Eels.' The word 'quadrille' often described these 'hot' dancing songs. Pianist Willie 'The Lion' Smith also wrote about Walton 'One-Leg Shadow' Gould, whom Ethel Waters also mentioned in her biography, one of the first to rag schottisches and quadrilles from the time of the civil war. Southern also mentions 'Old Man' Sam Moore, who was ragging some

23

quadrilles and schottisches in Philadelphia before 1875. Pianist The Shadow, born in Philadelphia in 1875, also mentioned "'Old Man' Sam Moore was ragging the quadrilles and schottisches before I was born." He added, "[h]e was born way before the war. He doubled on bass and piano." Continuing this interview with Blesh, he sat at the piano and played 'Sissie and Bob' pointing out this "Virginia reel is over 90 years old." On completion, he informed Blesh, "[o]h, they danced in them days and there was plenty ragtime." As confirmed by Scott Joplin in 1913: "There has been ragtime music in America ever since the Negro race has been here, but the white people took no notice of it until about twenty years ago." Since the minstrel days, music publishers covered spirituals, but in the 1890s, with the 'coon song' trend, they were taking an interest in other popular African American kinds of music. It mainly started with banjo instruction manuals, but as in the case of Sam Lucas, artists also understood the value of song publication as promotional material, and ragtime music was the next craze to come.[153-155]

Sheet music for ragtime pieces offered a multitude of African American depictions. Although it is easy to see that many are almost caricatures, many motions represented also appeared in more realistic drawings and paintings. Some of these motions, with kicking legs and high arms, seem to fit buck dance, Juba, and Cakewalk descriptions very well.

If looking at sheet music helps us focus on specific artists and some pictorial depictions, early records are of little help. As we have seen, military bands were often hired for social functions but could not be properly recorded on early cylinders. These string and brass bands provided the music for most social dances and performances. Newspapers of the time help us understand the social implication of emerging ragtime music. Some examples allow us to have a general idea of the scenes at the time.

In 1889, in Charleston, South Carolina, the Twin Brothers' Band played on two guitars, a fiddle, a mouth organ, and a 'call bell.' They provided "delightful music." The writer added lines about the band's technique: "He manipulated the guitar by a stick tied up to his stump. The violinist imitated the mockingbird to perfection." The article ended by informing the readers they could hire the band for balls and dance schools.[159]

Two years later, in Knoxville, Tennessee, "Marringhill and McCorkle, the banjo wonders and song and dance artists" were a hit. In New York in 1892, there was Sutton's 'U.T.C.' Co. writing that "[o]ur 'auction scene,' introducing banjo playing, laughing songs, negro dancing and patting, is quite a feature." [160-161]

In Richmond, Virginia, Prof. Wendell Phillips Dabney had his Dabney and his Richmond Banjo and Guitar Club that played for Tom's Cabin and Uncle Remus's shows that included dances and songs. For the Tom's Cabin show, "Henry Braxton delighted the audience with his fantastic dancing," and "Messrs. James Washington and Lee Mar held the audience spellbound with their song and dance act." In Uncle Remus, there was also "dancing by Mr. James Washington and Henry Braxton." [162]

In New York, "Mr. and Mrs. Al. E. Anderson, of the 'Slavery Days' Co., report having met with success since the opening of the season. Mr. Anderson has produced a new big four song and dance, entitled 'Four Night Ramblers,' introducing Jerry Mills, Henry Winfred, and Frank Sutton. The act consists of tumbling and high kicking." In 1894, in *Slavery Days*, "Alberta Monette caps the climax in her buck and wing dance." [163-164]

The same year, *Down in Dixie* was a new play with "Southern hoe downs by youthful colored dancers," a young African American band, and the Florida Quartette. "In one scene, a little coon who is busily engaged in finishing a watermelon drops into a stream and is swallowed by a monster alligator." The show *Old Kentucky* included the Pickaninny Band, also described as a juvenile brass band that did some dancing, and featured the "soft shoe dancing of Burt Grant." [165-166]

In Shelbyville, Kentucky, "Tom Martin's band was out in the west end serenading Saturday night ...the Shelby Cornet Band rendered music at the Bellevue house for those who delight in dancing." In New York a social dance moved to the music of J. M. Becker's Brass Band and, the following year, to Prof. Craig's orchestra. [167-168]

Still in New York City in 1892, references to the Topsy minstrel character or the term shouters, were also in use. To the music of E. O. Rogers, whose wife played Topsy, the show consisted of the "usual amount of dogs, ponies, donkeys," and was carried by "a colored concert company of twelve singers, shouters, dancers, etc.." On steamboats in 1892 in Georgia, the "Hill City string band and dancing was the leading feature." In 1893, in Mexico, Missouri, the Mexico Cornet band offered the music for plenty of dancing from the crowd. [169-171]

Back in Topeka in 1894, "dancing was the principal feature of the evening. The music was furnished by Atkinson & Dennis' mandolin club of Topeka." A few months later, with the same mandolin club, "about fifty couples entered the dancing hall, marched around the room several times and took their positions for dancing . . . They danced until about 10:30, and then the young ladies and their escorts had thirty minutes for supper, after which they danced until 1:45 A.M.." The Manitou Mandolin Club entertained a private dancing party in Ohio. Around the same time, the Jackson Military band also played for social dances. [172-174]

In 1894, at Froth Smith, Arkansas, the Junior Brass Band played 'After the Ball.' "Dancing was then indulged in until the arrival of the train at 2 A.M.." The band also joined the Heyer Colored Comedy Company, where Florence Hines and buck dancer Henry Williams worked for the show *Slavery Days*. [175]

Some dancers had already reached local fame, such as Sam Williams in Georgia, a six foot six inch giant who "performs a few tricks and is a song and dance artist, when not working in the field" in 1889. The Topeka press wrote about the famous little Harry Dillard around 1894. On a sadder note from 1895, "Tim Thompson, a little Negro boy, was asked to dance for the amusement of some white toughs. He refused, saying he was a church member. Jim Sosling, one of the men, knocked him down with a club, then danced upon his prostrate form. He then shot the boy in the hips. The boy is dead and the murderer is at large." As just seen, dancing was sometimes related to unfortunate experiences. At that time, the word 'rags' was used to describe some social dances, like in Topeka, Kansas, where "The Jordan hall 'rags,' which are held in Tennessee town weekly, are a nuisance and should be abated." [176-179]

There seemed to have been some racial conflicts around the Excelsior Reed and Brass Band in 1889. Tensions rose between a band member and the white-controlled Musical Association, which worked partly as a booking agency, when a dancer sued a white 'dancing master' who refused to accept her in her class because of her skin color. Fortunately, some entertainers reached a better fate.[180]

At an 1889 performance, there was mention of a string band show with banjo, violin, guitar, clappers, and a young dancer. "You should have seen the way that baby danced the shuffle, double and single, the curving and twisting of the body, the running on the heels, the side step, the back step, in fact all kinds of steps, that would have done credit to a minstrel performer." That young dancer had everything needed to enter the subsequent decades of dancing.[181]

An 1895 article in the Leavenworth Herald shared disappointment about the new dances, while showing that ragtime music was in between two eras; the music could relate to newer refined dancing, while it still had strong rural connotations. "The old time 'rag' dance is dying out. Nearly every thing which is done nowadays is called 'Modern,' which means that a thing is not near so good as it is when done in a way to designate that it is ancient. After all, a great many things that are called modern are really things that are ancient, polished over cunningly. People dance with a little more grace nowadays and wear finer clothes, and put on more airs, but they are probably less interesting than the old timers. It is alright to gaze upon a pretty woman, dressed becomingly, dancing with some gallant knight, or it may possibly look beautiful to see them executing the waltz, but it is much more interesting and amusing to see a coarser pair of individuals doing the Mobile buck, or the wide open shuffle, or the pigeon wing, or the break down. Before we die we want to attend a country 'rag' dance and see the people 'chasse,' 'balance all,' etc. We want to hear the caller, we want to hear the patting of hands, and then we will die happy, because we will know that our last desire has been fulfilled." At a grand ball of the Buckskin Club held in North Leavenworth, Kansas, on Christmas Eve, "After supper the round and square dances began. That ever favorite dance, the 'possum a la,' was introduced, and it seemed to carry the house by storm. The orchestra, which was composed of three pieces, a fiddle, bass fiddle a triangle, dispensed beautiful and melodious airs, which were fetching." [183]

A drastic paradigm shift came with the advent of the commercial recording industry. Without digging into details for the moment, the first decades of the cylinder records market focused primarily on waxing white artists, although exceptions existed. A valuable asset of the emerging record industry is that it allows us to follow the impact of some songs over the following decades. The desired characteristic to underline and follow here is the importance of ragtime sheet music as a vehicle for dance instructions and promotion, and that is why there will be a small jump in time in our narrative.

Jim Jackson was a medicine show guitarist and dancer born somewhere between 1876 and 1890 who played for local parties and dances with other Memphis musicians like Gus Cannon and Frank Stokes. He toured with the Silas Green Minstrels and, in 1905, with the Rabbit Foot Minstrels. His recording career only started for Vocalion in 1927. Jackson recorded some of his material, like 'Goin' to Kansas City,' which was an instant hit, and a variety of older tunes dating as far back as the previous century, like 'He's in the Jailhouse Now.' One of his prolific 8th recording session songs is 'Bye, Bye,Policeman,' the story of a craps player returning from a dance evening. Jackson mentions a set of dances and motions dating from previous decades, during the ragtime era: Bombashay, the World's Fair, the Turkey Trot, and the Pas-a-Ma-La. Dancer Ida Forsyne described The World's Fair; "you put your both foot together and move forward on your toes." White composer Max Hoffman wrote 'The Bom-ba-shay' song in 1897, and according to the lyrics, it is supposedly a Honolulu song. The dance also appeared in William Jerome's 'That Spooney Dance' (mentioning the Spooney, the Conney, and the Bombashay). Later, Ed Rogers and Saul Aarons said in a song that the Salome dance, the Cubanola, Pas'mala, and Bombashay are nothing compared to the Alabama Bound. Other white artists, Murphy and Wenrich, published a 'Baltimore Bombashay' in 1909, and African American composers and lyricists Creamer and Layton also published a Bombashay in 1916. A tap dance step also shares the name Bombershays.[183-184]

Jackson's song 'Bye, Bye, Policeman' mentioned one of the most popular dances from the ragtime music of the 1890s; The Pas Ma La. African American Irving Jones published the 'Possumala Dance' in 1893, a composition sometimes credited for its early syncopation with lyrics describing a social dance. In 1927, Jones, responding to an article in *The Birth of Jazz*, claimed he had invented Jazz when he put Pas Ma La dance on paper. Jones said, "I want to say that I was the first to write syncopated music. My music was published in 1893, and the song was called 'Pas Ma La Dance.' I tried every first class orchestra leader in the East to have it taken down from my voice, but none of them knew anything about ragtime music, and could not understand the unusual syncopated style . . ." White musicians sometimes recorded Jones' compositions around the turn of the century, but not the Pas-Ma-La.[185-186]

The song leads us to another famous performer of the time. Ernest Hogan was born in Kentucky in 1865 and worked for the minstrel troupe The Georgia Graduates as a musician, dancer, and composer. Participating in the ragtime craze, he published the song 'All Coons Look Alike to Me' in 1895, but just before that, he published a version of 'Pas-Ma-La' for his piece *In Old Tennessee*. Sterns describes the dance as the transition between folk and topical dances of the time. It contained the following instructions: "Fus yo say 'my nigah' git yo' gun, shoot a dem ducks and away yo run, Now my little coon come 'a down the shute with the St-Louis Pass and Chicago Salute. Hand upon yo' head, let your mind roll far, Back, back, back and look at the stars. Stand up rightly, and dance it brightly. That's the Pas Ma La." In the second chorus, we find the line "Fus yo say 'my nigah' Bombisha, then turn 'round and go the other way, to the World's Fair and do the Turkey Trot." The World's Fair in the lyrics refers to the Chicago World's Fair of 1893; an important exhibition also referred to as a dance movement in Jackson's song.[187-188]

In 1903, an article gave a version of Hogan's inspiration for the song. Hogan was playing piano for a dance in Kansas City, where a quadrille caller named 'The Swell of New Orleans' did well until calling 'Pas.' A French word for 'step,' the caller was not understood, causing confusion; 'Ma La' is close to the French for confused, and someone said it was the newest dance craze. Hogan used it, then made an orchestration when touring for his show *In Old Tennessee*. This quadrille became a favorite at the influential Forty Drops dance club, where Marches, Polkas, and the likes were less and less popular.[189-190]

Isaac Goldberg followed the idea that the name of the vernacular dance could come from the french 'pas mele' (mixed step), found, for instance, in the 1895 sheet music for 'La Das Pas Malaise' (The Difficult Step). Irving Berlin's 'Possumala' theme is also the second part of the piece of 'I Meet Dat Coon Tonight' by Blind Boone in 1892. The second section is named 'dance' and is left as an instrumental segment. In 1895, the 'Pamala' was also described as a "weird negro gliding dance." A 'Real Coon Rag' around 1914 contains elements of dance instructions traceable to the Pas Ma La. There was also another dance, clearly inspired by the Pas Ma La, at least in the name, that also bears similar indications to various other dances of the time. The 'Shaw's Rag-Ma-Pa' explained to "S'lute your babies all, Hotfoot it down the hall, give your honey the inside track, now do the Palmer House coming back, and the Wenches Chain, swing around again, back to place, with due grace, that's the rag-a-ma-la." [191-195]

Many musicians and dancers from the jazz era remembered the dance. Henry 'Rubberlegs' Williams saw it performed by young African American performers working with white vaudeville star Nora Bayes. Walter Crumbley confirmed the Pas Ma La was a comedy dance, while Perry Bradford said it "consisted of a series of fast, flat hops." [196-197]

The Pas Ma La dance also led to a series of variations, especially if we consider also the 'Possum' dances related to it. At Madison Square Garden in New York City, a prominent touring show near the turn of the century, the Isham's Octoroons, featured the Alabama Possumala. Under the name 'Possum Up a Gum Tree,' it appears in the publication *Georgia Scenes* (1835) by Augustus Longstreet, and in 1834 in 'Zip Coon' as a song. Eileen Southern mentioned that actor Ira Aldridge (1807-1867) went to the British Isles and sang 'Opposum Up a Gum,' which Southern also identifies as coming from a 'slave song,' a repertory still very present indeed during Aldridge's lifetime. In 1893, a dance master in Louisville, Kentucky, warned his students about the Possum dance around the same time as Irving Jones and Ernest Hogan's publications.[198-199]

Trombonist Clyde Bernhardt mentioned Carrie Adams, part of blues singer Ma Rainey's show, was singing 'Tree and a Possum' "with all that hound dog mocking that the people liked." This testimony confirms Walter Crumbley's comment about it being a comical dance. With a similar name, we also have the description of the 'Possum Walk,' described by comic dancer and actor Pigmeat Markham as "two or three steps forward and then two or three quick jumps back." [200-201]

Back on records, Jim and Andrew Baxter recorded 'Dance the Georgia Poss' on guitar and violin for Victor in 1927 in North Carolina, a year before Jim Jackson was recording 'Bye, Bye, Policeman' in Memphis. Baxter was a fiddle player born in 1869, so like Jackson, he witnessed the ragtime dance craze in his youth. The lyrics went, "it's the newest dance in town," describing it as "get way back, hold your gal, get way back and fall." It bears almost the exact same melody as Hogan's 'Pas Ma La.' A few years later, John Lomax recorded a little girl, Anne Brewer, in Alabama, in 1937, singing 'Possom-a-la.' It instructs the dancer to put the hands on the hips and let the mind roll forward, back, back, back, until you see the stars. Then skip lightly and shine brightly. These are all included in Ernest Hogan's version of 1895.[202]

The recorded version of Georgia Sea Island-based Bessie Jones of 'Old Bill Rolling Pin' is a game song with a storytelling part including swimming motions and reference to hitting a stick and not being able to do anything but the possum-la. Bessie Jones also knew a step similar to the knee bend with the same name. "The 'Possum-La' dance shuffles and 'cuts up' casually, or perhaps skips around in a circle, until the word 'possum-la,' when he gives a slight jump, or 'chug,' to one side, landing with his knees deeply bent. The same action is taken on the word 'seed.' In the refrain, the dancer makes five such jumps, swinging his body from side to side and jumping first at one angle and then at another one." New Orleans guitarist Snooks Eaglin recorded the song 'Possum Up a Gum Tree' as late as 1958 with Percy Randolph on the washboard and the singing voice of Lucious Bridges.[203-204]

Henry Tuvillon had been the boss of a railway section gang, a levee worker, and a dock labourer in Mississippi. He recorded for John Lomax and Ruby T. Lomax in 1940 in Burkeville, Texas. His session included "'Come On Boys, Let's Go to Huntin," which mentioned 'Possum Up the Gum Tree.' Another peculiar related appearance can be found in a discussion on log loading and singing that includes the version 'Racoon Up a Gum Tree,' recorded by Bruce Jackson in a Texas prison in 1966.[205]

Jackson's song demonstrates many essential components to remember while reviewing records for dance references. First, we need to recall performers were often gifted dancers, and their practice might go back years before the recording date. In this case, Jackson might have performed the Possumala as a kid decades before leaving its trace on records. Then, a dance occurrence does not imply the dance was limited to a specific subculture. In this case, the song links it to dance halls around Memphis. At the same time, history shows links to slavery, other dances in main urban centers, blues stage performances with Ma Rainey, and game songs still active into the 60s on the Georgia coastal islands with Bessie Jones.

Performer Tom Fletcher helped to put the importance of the Pas Ma La dance in its time. He wrote, "Besides the Cake-Walk, a new dance, the Pasumala, and another, the Black Annie, came into existence. These new dances were good and they enjoyed some popularity, but none of them ever surpassed, or even equalled, the popularity of the Cake-Walk which became an international favorite." [206]

1- Ruhiere around 1830   2- The Old Plantation, late 18th century   3- Francis Johnson   4- In Ole Virginny (1876)   5- Master Juba   6- Howard Helmick -The Juba Dance (1895)

DANCING FOR EELS.

A Scene from the New Play of NEW-YORK AS IT IS, as played at the Clatham Theatre, N. Y.

1- Dance representations in various drawings   2- Dancing for Eels

The Georgia Minstrels

C. H. SMITH'S DOUBLE MAMMOTH
UNCLE TOM'S CABIN CO.

SAM . LUCAS
COLORED COMEDIAN

1- Charles Barney Hicks   2- Lew Johnson   3- Lew Johnson   4 and 5- Sam Lucas

Original North Carolina Slaves Troupe

BILLY KERSANDS.
CALLENDER'S (GEORGIA) MINSTRELS.

1- Anna Madah Hyers   2- Emma Louise Hyers   3 and 4- Bily Kersands

1- Dancing by the River   2- Dancing in Congo Square by Edward Winsor Kemble (1886)
3- Music sheet by Rolling Howard   4- The Fisk Jubilee Singers

ZONDAGSBLAD

van de

Amsterdamsche Courant.

Abonnement

Voor Amsterdam per 3 maanden . . . . ƒ 0.40.
Buitenland . . . . 0.55.
Voor geabonneerden op de *Amsterdamsche Courant* gratis.

Zondag 10 Mei. — No. 122

Advertentiën

van 1—5 regels . . . . ƒ 1.—.
Elke regel meer . . . . 0.20.
Groote letters naar plaatsruimte.
Kantoor: DE BRAKKE GROND, Nos 53.

1896. — 3e Jaargang.

De „Fisk Jubilee Singers."

Mrs. THOMAS — I. Sopraan.

Mrs. MAGGIE COLE. — I. Sopraan.

Miss CORA COLE. — Contra Alt.

CH. S. BYRON — Trial

J. JOHNSTONE — I. Bas

CH. LEWIS. — I. Tenor.

N. CALDWELL. — II. Bas.

CH. PAYNE — II. Tenor.

1- The Fisk Jubilee Singers (1887)   2- Queen City Band around 1886   3- Irving Jones

1- Jame Well Champney, 'A Jolly Ratfull -Taking the Flood Good-Naturally,' (1883) 2- Howard Weeden, 'Dancing in the Sun' (1900) 3- Giorgiana Davis, 'Courtyard of a Rice Mill. The Noob Hour' (1883)

1- Edward Windsor Kemble, 'In the Store,' (1887) 2- Howard Helmick, Uncle Henson Cuts the Pigeon Wing,' (1897)

1- Arthur Burdett Frost, 'There's Music in the air,' Wood engraving, (1879) 2- W.E. Mears, 'Celebrating Chirstma,' (1911)

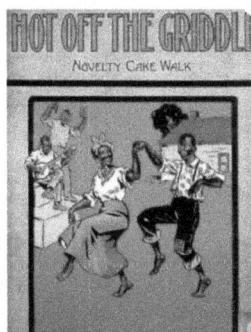

1- Willard Poinsette Snyder, 'Some One Produced a Fiddle, and They Danced,' (1884) 2- William Woodlow Sheppard, 'Dinner-Time at the Tobacco-Factory' (1870) 3- W.W. Sheppard. 'The Dance,' (1882) 4- Music sheet

1- Ernest Hogan   2- Ira Aldridge   3- J.W. Otto, 'Make a Pretty Motion,' (1901)

1-The Georgia Minstrels in the 1870s   2-The Original Georgia Minstrel and Alabama Cakewalkers around 1899

1- The Different Four   2- Oriental Company

Iring Sayles, performer with the Hicks-Sawyers Minstrels

Next Page: Irving Sayles

Images are a courtesy of the Library of Congress, the New York Public Library, the Schomburg Center, the Helen Armstead-Johnson Photograph Collection, the Emory archives, Yale University, newspapers, private collections

Notes

1. Malone, p. 144
2. Gaunt, p. 3
3. Hazzard-Gordon, p. 6-7, and Geroge Howe, "The Last Slave-Ship." Scribner's Magazine, July 1890, 123-124-114
4. Ibid, p. 12
5. Ibid, p. 18-19
6. Floyd, *Power of Black Music*, p. 53
7. Stearns, p. 20
8. Ibid, p. 24
9. Southern, *The Music of Black Americans: A History*, p. 108-115
10. Southern, *Images: Iconography of Music In African-American Culture, 1770s-1920s*, p. 17
11. Southern, *Images: Iconography of Music In African-American Culture, 1770s-1920s*, p. 20
12. Ibid, p. 70
13. Ibid, p. 32
14. Ibid, p. 68
15. Ibid, p. 67
16. Ibid, p. 68-69
17. Jordan Heckscher, p. 22, from Malning
18. Ibid, p. 28
19. Hazzard-Gordon, p. 24, from Abe C. Ravity, "John Pierpont and the slaves' Christmas," *Phylon* 21 (Winter 1960):384
20. Oliver, *Off the Records; Thirty Years of Blues Commentary*, p. 27
21. Talley, p. 1
22. White and White, p. 48
23. Ibid, p. 49-50
24. Allen, p. 14
25. Ibid, p. 15
26. Ibid, p.121
27. Defrantz educational video for Duke University
28. Allen, p. 221
29. Southern, *Images: Iconography of Music In African-American Culture, 1770s-1920s*
30. Lhamon, p. 27
31. Ibid,p. 10
32. Ibid, p. 30-31
33. Ibid, p. 33
34. Emery, p. 190 and Abbott, *Out of Sight: The Rise of African American Popular Music:1889-1895*, p. 374
35. Haskins, p. 17
36. Abbott and Seroff, *Out of Sight: The Rise of African-American Popular Music:1889-1895*, p. 374
37. Smith, p. 178
38. Ibid, p. 36
39. Fletcher,p. 18
40. Southern, *Images: Iconography of Music In African-American Culture, 1770s-1920s*, p. 31
41. Lane, p. 14
42. Smith, p. 167, from Olive Lewin and Maurice G. Gordon
43. Taylor and Austin, p. 40
44. Ibid, p. 5
45. Emery, p. 194
46. Bradford, p. 30
47. Toll, p. 198
48. Ibid, p. 201
49. Abbott and Seroff, *Ragged but Right*, p. 7
50. Toll, p. 198
51. Herzhaft, p. 204
52. Toll, p. 206-212
53. Fletcher, p. 39
54. Sampson, *Blacks in Blackface*, p. 2299

55. Ibid, p. 1300
56. J.W. Johnson, p. 91 and Toll, p. 217
57. Graham, p. 232
58. Ibid, p. 215
59. Ibid, p. 217
60. *New York Age*, 12 Dec. 1885. The Songs of Sam Lucas - The Songs (mtsu.edu)
61. Fletcher,p. 71 and 76
62. Sampson, *Blacks in Blackface*, p. 2288)
63. Ibid, p. 1830
64. Ibid, p. 231
65. Ibid, p. 461
66. Toll, p. 217
67. Sampson, *Blacks in Blackface*, p. 1299
68. Fletcher, p. 7
69. Sampson, *Blacks in Blackface*, p. 2296
70. Ibid, p. 1539
71. Ibid, p. 1991-1992
72. J.W. Johnson, p. 89
73. Sampson, *Blacks in Blackface*,p. 2296
74. Stearns, p. 51
75. Sampson, *Blacks in Blackface*, p. 1991
76. Fletcher, p. 10 and 12
77. Ibid, p. 61
78. Hogan Archives Interview and Stearns, p. 51
79. Graham, p. 17
80. Ibid,p. 88-89
81. Ibid, p. 91-92
82. Ibid,p. 100 and 106
83. Ibid, p. 225
84. Ibid, p. 118
85. Ibid, p. 125
86. Ibid, p. 108
87. Ibid, p. 210
88. Ibid, p. 214
89. Ibid, p. 174
90. Ibid, p. 233 and 235-236
91. Ibid, p. 247
92. Ibid, p.167
93. Ibid, p. 182
94. Ibid, p. 168
95. Ibid, p. 199
96. Ibid, p. 126
97. Ibid, p. 133
98. ibid, p. 135
99. Ibid, p. 141
100. Ibid, p. 146 and Abbott and Seroff, *Out of Sight*, p. 186 and 189
101. Abbott and Seroff, *Out of Sight,* p. 186 and 189
102. Ibid, 238-239
103. Ibid, p. 247
104. Ibid, p. 247
105. Ibid, p. 259
106. McCuster, p. 82
107. Emery, p. 21-29
108. By Moreau de St-Mery, Courlander, *Negro Folk Music, U.S.A.*, p. 191
109. Ibid,p. 191
110. Emery, p. 39
111. Ibid, p. 27
112. Hersch, p. 144
113. Ibid,p. 145
114. Herzhaft, *American Music*, p. 116
115. Emery, p. 71
116. Hersch, p. 20
117. Ibid, p. 17
118. Ibid, p. 17

119. Ibid, p. 21
120. Turner, p. 14
121. Kmen, p. 227
122. Emery, p. 156
123. Goffin, *La Nouvelle-Orléans, capitale du jazz*, p. 29
124. Emery, p. 164
125. Southern, *Images: Iconography of Music In African-American Culture, 1770s-1920s*, p. 36
126. Blesh, *Shining Trumpets*, p. 83
127. Ibid, p. 83
128. Buerkle, p. 12
129. Blesh, *Shining Trumpets*, p. 84
130. Alger, p. 23
131. Blesh, *Shining Trumpets*, p. 35
132. Kmen, p. 229
133. Kmen, and Bethel, p. 6
134. Goffin, *La Nouvelles-Orléans, capitale du jazz*, p. 33
135. Smith, p. 47-48
136. Bechet, p. 9
137. Ibid, p. 51-52
138. Kmen, p. 43
139. Ibid, p. 230
140. Ibid, p. 43-47
141. Ibid, p. 49-50
142. Ibid, p. 52
143. Hazzard-Gordon, p. 51 and 53
144. Ibid, p. 56
145. Ibid, p. 60
146. Kmen, p. 239-241 and Smith, p. 48
147. Wondrich, p. 106
148. Ibid, p. 108-109 and Abbot, *Out of Sight*, p. 58
149. Abbott, Out of Sight, 58
150. Bradford, p. 53 and Chrisopher J. Smith, *The Creolization of American Culture*, 2013, and Handy's interview with Lomax
151. Abbott and Seroff, *Out of Sight*, p. 428
152. Waldo, p. vii
153. Floyd, p. 67
154. Southern, *The Music of Black Americans: A History, p. 124*
155. Smith, *Music on My Mind*, p. 67
156. Souther, *The Music of Black Americans: A History*, p. 310
157. Blesh, *Shining Trumpets*, p. 190
158. Curtis, *Joplin*, p. 47
159. Abbott and Seroff, *Out of Sight*, p. 57
160. Ibid, p. 182
161. Ibid, p. 242
162. Ibid, p. 251-252
163. Ibid, p. 305
164. Ibid, p. 366
165. Ibid, p. 348
166. Ibid, p. 407-408
167. Ibid, p. 192
168. Ibid, p. 201 and 221
169. Ibid, p. 131
170. Ibid, p. 232
171. Ibid, p. 303
172. Ibid, p. 248
173. Ibid, p. 248
174. Ibid, p. 401
175. Ibid, p. 338-339
176. Ibid, p. 50
177. Ibid, p. 399
178. Ibid, p. 419
179. Ibid, p. 201
180. Ibid, p. 263
181. Ibid, p. 48, from Florence Williams, *New York Age*
182. Ibid. p.444

183. Stearns, p. 101
184. Jasen, p. 364
185. Abbott and Seroff, *Out of Sight,*, p. 444
186. Ibid, p. 444
187. Stearns, p. 119
188. Abbott and Seroff, *Out of Sight,*, p. 445
189. Ibid, p. 444
190. Southern, *The Music of Black Americans; A History*, p. 315
191. Abbott and Seroff, *Out of Sight: The Rise of African American Popular Music: 1889-1895, p. 447*
192. Riis,p. 179
193. Blesh, *Shining Trumpets*, p. 87
194. Abbott, out, p. 444
195. Idib, p. 451
196. Stearns, p. 83
197. Ibid, p. 101
198. Southern, *The Music of Black Americans; A History*, p. 120
199. Abbott and Seroff, *Out of Sight*, p. 444
200. Bernhardt, p. 26
201. Stearns, p. 67
202. Abbott and Seroff, *Out of Sight,*, p. 447
203. Jones and Lomax, p. 127
204. Snooks Eaglin, *Country Boy in New Orleans*, Arhoolie records, liner notes
205. *Wake Up Dead Man*, liner notes
206. Fletcher, p. 43

Chapter two: the Cakewalk

The list of dances from the ragtime era would not be complete without the Cakewalk. It was the leading dance to go through a transition from the plantations to the minstrel stage and ragtime sheet music The dance started on the plantation as a contest where the winning dancing couple would win a cake offered by the slave owners. Shephard N. Edmonds confirmed banjo music accompanied the dance before reaching the minstrel stage. As much as the dance was a demonstration of skills, it was also a parody of white behaviors and dancing. Abraham wrote, "[s]o we find in the Cakewalk a mimicry of the white cotillion through an exaggeration of European-style walking, parading, and dancing with the hypercorrect throwing back of the shoulders and head, and the exaggerated forward march of those white swells on parade." Throwing back the head in an exaggerated fashion until you see the stars is a motion also part of the Pas Ma La routine.[1-2]

Similar testimony came from an ex-slave from South Carolina; "[u]s slaves watched white folks' parties where the guests danced a minuet and then paraded in a grand march, with the ladies and gentlemen doing different ways and then meeting up again, arm in arm, and marching down the center together," "[t]hen we'd do it too, but we used to mock 'em, every step. Sometimes the white folks noticed it, but they seemed to like it; I guess they thought we couldn't dance any better." Ethel L. Urlin proposed in his *Dancing, Ancient and Modern* (1912) that the Cakewalk might also come from Florida, where Black people imitated the Seminole war dances where they participated as spectators and dancers, jumping and gyrating alternated with solemn couple walk. The Cakewalk done at harvest balls included the restriction to walk on a chalk line, which also justified the name of 'chalk-line walk.'[3-4]

Tom Fletcher wrote about the time the Cakewalk was not yet a stage dance. "Sometimes on pleasant evenings, boards would be laid down for an impromptu stage before the verandah so the guests could have a good view of the proceedings and a real shindig would take place with singing and dancing. The cake walk, in that section and at that time, was known as the chalk line walk. There was no prancing, just a straight walk on a path made by turns and so forth, along which the dancers made their way with a pail of water on their heads. The couple that was the most erect and spilled the least water or no water at all was the winner." "'Son,' said my grandfather, 'your grandmother and I, we won all of the prizes and were taken from plantation to plantation. The dance became a great fad. It took skill and good nerves. Our sizes were well balanced, everybody said, and we made a good couple to be called the champions. We'd have these dancing contests and a watermelon contest, and the singing would round out the evening...The plantation is where shows like yours first started, son,' he said." Roger Abrahams mentioned the dance was also named the walkaround and the strut.[5-6]

Some perennial American songs were written primarily for the minstrel shows' walkaround finale, such as 'Oh, Susanna,' written by Stephen Foster for the Christy's Minstrel show in 1848, and 'Dixie' by Dan Emmet for Bryant's Minstrel in 1860. While these composers were white, African Americans also wrote some walkaround songs.[7]

James A. Bland was born in New York in 1854 to an African American middle-class family, but he grew up in Washington. He was playing refined versions of ex-slaves' songs on the banjo. His earliest known stage presence was with the Original Black Diamonds in Boston in 1875. He became a popular feature of minstrel shows and composed 'Carry Me Back to Old Virginny,' a song popular since the 1840s and sung during the war. Bland's version, lyrically nostalgic of the plantation days, was popular when African Americans struggled to find work after emancipation. The song lasted long in the popular repertoire, including a Ray Charles version on his album *Sings for America*. Another of Bland's compositions from 1879 became the definitive walkaround piece: 'Oh, Dem Golden Slippers.' This song also lasted a while in musicians' repertoire since Fats Waller recorded a lively version in 1939. Another Bland composition, 'In the Evening by the Moonlight,' was recorded by Nina Simone. Bland wrote over 700 songs over his career.

Bland's composition 'Dancing on the Kitchen Floor' (1880) also provides images of a house party of the time: "[o]h how happy everyone will be. As we dance on the kitchen floor," and mentions that at the 'darkies jubilee,' "[t]here'll be walking for the cake, all the ladies hearts we'll break, when we all commence to do the promenade."

James Bland joined Haverly's Genuine Colored Minstrels in 1879 alongside two famous African American comedians; Billy Kersands and Sam Lucas. In the 1880s, he moved to Europe to perform for the next 20 years. Coming back from Europe, Bland continued to perform on stage, and W. C. Handy recalled him in the Black Patti Troubadours and played some of his songs at Carnegie Hall in 1928. His career declined, though, and pianist Eubie Blake recalled one time when they met at a bar in Atlantic City and Bland escaped without paying for his drinks.[8]

The walkaround became integrated into white minstrel shows, like the Harrigan and Hart's Cordelia's Aspiration, which included a segment entitled 'Sam Johnson's Cakewalk' in 1883, or the Passing Show with "a dozen colored folks" doing the plantation dance. One of the most prominent figures of early African American shows claims to have brought it to the stage, even if it was probably already a common feature of minstrelsy.[9]

Billy McClain was born in Indianapolis in 1866. He played the cornet in George Bell's Band and joined Lew Johnson's Minstrels in 1883 before moving to various minstrel shows and circuses. Tom Fletcher wrote he was "[o]ne of the outstanding old time minstrel men, musicians and actors of the early years in show business." [10]

Proud of his achievement, Billy McClain penned an article entitled 'Billy McClain—Originator of the Cake Walk' for the *Indianapolis Freeman* newspaper in 1910, in which he relates parts of his story. "Dan Palmer and I were the first colored acrobats and trapeze performers out of Indianapolis. Later, with Cleveland's Minstrels, Tom Brown and I were the first to do a sketch of a Chinaman and a 'coon' in Kansas City in 1887 at the Gaiety Theater, where the colored performers' reputation extended from Walnut Street to Independence Avenue, an area of ten blocks." McClain also shared the stage with the Hyers Sisters, who had worked with Sam Lucas. Tom Fletcher described them as "two beautiful colored girls with very good voices and versatility" who "organized a company that was different from minstrel shows." It still presented the famous dance, though. McClain continued his article by claiming, "I was the first to put a cake walk on the stage, with the Hyers Sisters. Harry Stafford was with the show and I introduced him to Anna Hyers. Then I called it a 'walk around.' After that I produced it with the South before the War and called it the 'cake walk.' It has become famous all over the world." [11-13]

McClain was also interested in promoting other dances, such as his 1893 new song and dance of the 'Old School House Bells,' performed by Katie Carter and praised in his minstrel's shows. Not much is known about Katie Carter, but Abbott states she was a specialist in vernacular dances and a member of Curtis' Afro-American Specialty Company touring Australia in 1899. [14]

One of the interesting early rare birds of the Cakewalk, both as a social dancer and show dancer, was a female impersonating cakewalker. Born into slavery in 1858, William Dorsey Swann started organizing balls in Washington and labeled himself the Queen of Drag. At the ball, other men, including his brother, dressed in silk to dance at the ball. On many occasions, police raided his balls as early as 1888, and years later, he was jailed for running a brothel. One of the dances he performed was the Cakewalk. [15]

The term Cakewalk was also a general indication for a social dance in which, usually, a Cakewalk contest was inserted. There were student Cakewalk dances, like those at the Hampton Institute in Virginia in the 1880s. Some contests could start at midnight, and the social dance would finish in the morning, like the one won in 1889 by Belle Wilson and George Thompson with second prize going to Mary Washington and Samuel Stewart. [16-17]

For these, there must have been hundreds of amazing dancers winning contests all over the country. Only a few names have survived, like Edward Banks and Elizabeth White in 1888, J. Gould and G.W. Miller in 1890, or Cole Shelton and Stella Berry in 1896. [18-19]

As in any social affairs, sometimes it was disappointing just how few dancers attended, like the three couples for the Colored People Day in Wilmington for a contest won by Cephus Finch and Haines Davis in 1892. Violent confrontations also took place in these dance events; in Baltimore in 1885, Henry Powell shot Mary

Frances Neal and assaulted Ellas Prescoe with a knife. In Evansville in 1889, John Fitzgerald gunned down a man who kissed his wife at the Cakewalk; the same year in New York, there were guns involved in an altercation between rivals at a Cakewalk, involving Willie and Eva Woods; in Leesburg, Adam Graves tried to kill Tom Pearson at a Cakewalk because Tom was dancing with the girl he liked, and some pushing and gunshots followed.[20-24]

Some problems arose when dancers wanted to hold a Cakewalk in a Brooklyn church during the night in 1888, and, still in Brooklyn eight years later, there was a riot because some did not agree on the winners of the waltz, part of the contest for the cane and umbrella prize: The "prizes were awarded to Jackson and his dusky partner. The decision of the judges made other competitors for the prizes jealous, and while the men jumped on Jackson and proceeded to play football with him, the women went for Jackson's partner and pulled her hair out and tore the clothes off her back." [25-26]

In Brooklyn in 1891, "the colored citizens were nearly driven into hysterical delight," by the Cakewalk. Some contestants were dismissed by the judges, some for their clothes, one for how he moved his limbs. As it often happened the social Waltz dancing was preliminary to the contest, sometimes even in the contest. Dandy Jack Smith won the prize "despite the fact that his checker-board trousers should have disqualified him" and the police had to be called about a fight for the second prize between Ayler (with his very unique style), Jackson and Colvin. The next year, Dandy Jack saw his name in an article's title for not winning the contest when, with Miss. Hoey, they were in third place behind C. Blackburn and Martha James, and William Proctor and Maud Clifford. In 1895, a man named Tom Brown won second place at a Cakewalk in Brooklyn; he was perhaps the famous performer of the same name. Another name from the Brooklyn Cakewalk scene from 1896 was "the old time cake-walker, Eddie Mann, who has a knack for winning all the fancy Cakewalks, and, of course, Eddie was at it again last night. It was demonstrated that as a cake-walker, he can't be beat." The Cakewalk started late in the evening, and there was also some buck dancing.[27-31]

The social dances often involved conflicts arising from the 'race' problem, although this was rarely discussed in the press. In 1891, there was a mixed couple in a contest, Pat Daly, white, 125 pounds, and Nettie Wright, colored, 250 pounds, for a contest won by Eldie Man and Miss Seman. There were also cases like that of Mrs. John Williams Mollenhauer, married to a sugar cane millionaire, who was relieved from the sacred union for "attending a negro cakewalk, danc[ing] with men of questionable reputation, and drank freely." There were also warnings of conspiracies that whites wanted to ban the Cakewalk contest, as expressed in an emotional speech held at the Limekiln Club in 1894.[32-34]

The contests themselves were serious business, and a description from 1892 in Louisville, Kentucky, gave a good example. The observer noticed, when the second couple, Len Sykes and Florence Richards competed, that the "expression on the faces of both of these contestants was firm and determined. Never a smile loosened the muscles of their face, which were drawn as tightly as fiddle strings." Meanwhile, Willie Wilkins, the male from the third couple, suffered from stage fright, unnoticed by his partner Ida S. Maye.

When the couples went into the promenade, "Mr. Miller had a game leg. That was clear when he turned. While going straight ahead, all was well, but ah! that fatal turn! The game leg got behind, and was several feet in catching up. Mr. Miller's bows, as he faced the audience, were most courtly. They were grand. The seep of his hand, the gentle collapse of his body, the recovery, were inimitable. Mr Miller's work was sprightly. There was a springy motion, an 'ah, there!' in his steps. It was the walk of a king, of a millionaire–until he turned. Mrs. Miller moved as serenely about the stage as a swallow on the wing. The painful hitoh [sic] in her husband's leg, when he turned, did not discomfit her. Her smile only increased. Then, when she bowed! There was poetry of motion. No ballroom belle ever saluted a friend more gracefully. It brought down the house, that bow."

Things were more complicated for the second couple; "Mr. Wilkins was in a hurry. His steps were short but nervous. He had grown reckless. He had forgotten the cake. He simply wanted to get off the stage and hide himself in some dark corner. When he bowed, he threatened to go all to pieces. It was a regular Eastern salaam. There was desperation written in that angular swing of the body. Miss Maye was indifferent. She tripped along as if she did not care if school kept her or not. One thing she noticed–that her partner was affected. However, she showed no sympathy for him." The next couple fared better.

"Mr. Archer Miles and Miss Georgia Bradley walked down the stage. Mr. Miles did not have a dress suit, no flowers, no cane, no silk hat, but the way he walked was a caution to dancing masters. Straight and true, silently as a ghost, gracefully as a deer, he came down to the footlights. Then he turned–'Ah! He's a winner!' cried the crowd–and without a balk or a mis-step made his way around the rear. There was a slight roll in his walk, just enough to make it smooth, to break off the corners. Miss Bradley was a complement to Mr. Miles. She filled out the style of perfect Cakewalk grace. Miss Bradley is not of a frivolous nature. She does not walk that way. There is a purpose, the realization of a future, of a world beyond this, in her walk. It was not heavy, it was not light -it was firm."

"When the next act of the cakewalk came, everybody was excited. The last promenade had come. The end was near. Mr. Miller and Mrs. Miller marched forth first. Mr. Miller's bow was deeper than before. He lifted his feet higher, and was stiffer about the neck. He knew the crucial test had come. He was giving the best style of walking he had in his shop. Mr. Miles and Miss Bradley showed up in fine form in the last heat. They glided down to the footlights, and they backed, then advanced, then wheeled, then turned, and the crowd named them the winners." The winners for the "free for all cakewalk" section were John Walker and Julia Tate; "the crowd liked his style and cheered his every step." [35]

Also in 1889, a Cakewalker named Caesar committed a mistake, "[h]e started off on the wrong foot. The whole audience noticed it, and while the judges frowned all knew that meant no cake for Caesar." The whole crowd expected Joseph Marshall Purcell, a "veteran cakewalker of seventy-five summers," to win. The judges decided otherwise, and after some complications, they split the cake in many parts in front of an applauding crowd.[36]

As briefly mentioned, minstrel shows and carnivals integrated the Cakewalk often in their finale scenes, a tradition kept alive even in the late 1890s. Born in 1879 in Iowa, Nettie Compton, known as 'The Bronze Eva Tanguay,' was performing the Cakewalk for the Ponsell Brothers circus as a teenager. "I can still see it--the girls kind of flirted, and the boys strutted and pranced." She explained: "You use a lot of strut in the Cakewalk–lots of fellows walked like that just for notoriety–and they could really show off. The girl would stop and applaud her partner, while he made up four steps of his own, sometimes regular tap steps, and then he'd end it, maybe with a somersault. We had some nice dancers and a good band." Richards & Pringle's, Rusco & Holland's Big Minstrel Festival's publicity of 1898, or Oliver Scott's Big Minstrel Carnival of 1899 confirm links between the Cakewalk, minstrels, and carnivals. Al W. C. Martin's *Uncle Tom's Cabin* production also integrated a Cakewalk presentation, while in 1901, A. Brady's show of *Uncle Tom's Cabin* gathered 200 cakewalkers. It was managed by Luke Pulley, a pianist and orchestra leader who also worked for *The South Before the War*.[37-38]

Some African American critics disliked the tradition of cake walking in the parodic minstrel shows, complaining it was no longer respectable. Nevertheless, the popularity of the Cakewalk on the stage led to a panoply of contests around the country. Publicity for the Primrose and West's Big Minstrels from 1896 shows elegant Africanm American dancers and invites dancers to participate in a competition. In Philadelphia, a big Cakewalk contest and show occurred at the Horticultural Hall and The Academy of Music in 1896-97. The Cakewalk Jubilee Contest at Madison Square Garden in 1895 lasted three days and included six thousand couples, mostly colored. It also had a male buck dance contest, a female wing dance contest, and the Grand Cakewalk.[39-40]

Poet Paul Dunbar disliked the Cakewalk demonstration for its vulgarity, an opinion shared by many prominent African Americans, and for a show at Madison Square Garden, he only liked the work of Mattie Wilkes (Hogan's wife). Still, he wrote that Billy Farrell and his wife were "worldbeaters, they had no competitor who could even be considered, unless it was Mr. and Mrs. Luke Blackburn."

Performer Tom Fletcher gave a detailed account of the competition there. "The Madison Square Garden competition was always a sellout. Before the contest, there would be a big plantation scene with the cast of about 150 singers and dancers and some great vocal soloists of the period. After this show was over, the judges, including many of New York's prominent brokers, sportsmen and athletes, especially prize fighters, would take their places on the stage. Walter F. Craig and his orchestra of fifty pieces would be seated on the stage to provide the music."

"The inside of Madison Square Garden on such occasions was arranged like a race track. The space for the Cake Walkers ran alongside the boxes and loges.

Chairs were placed on the floor to mark off the space for the contestants. When the contest music started, first would appear a drum major who would go through a routine with his baton then return to his place as leader. Then the curtain would part and 50 or 60 couples would come from behind the stage on to the floor, prancing and dancing to the tempo of the music. It was very reminiscent of the grand entry at a circus." [41]

"The girls' dresses were of all colors. The men wore full dress, clown clothes or comedy costumes with the big checks. When all the walkers were on the floor, then the 50 or 60 couples could all be seen doing different prances and dance steps ranging from buck-and-wing to toe dancing and, in fact, practically everything known to the terpsichorean art. As the couples went around the floor." [42]

"The ten best couples selected by the judges would be brought up on the stage to compete for the prizes and that is when the real big doings got underway. When the ten couples did their numbers around the stage, the audience could get a good look at them because when they were walking around the floor it was more like a big circus with three rings and two stages where something different was going on at the same time. With a chance to get a good look and pick a couple it liked best, the audience would make bets on the final winners, giving odds and all. A few of the couples would stick to the old style of the original Cake Walk. The best of the couples would receive a prize for their style." [43]

"Cake Walk winners were judged by time, style and execution. Mr. and Mrs. Luke Blackburn who did the original walk ran out of the competition. They became a big feature and would appear only to show the way the Cake Walk started. The younger people went for the new style. The couples that emerged winners or runners-up usually formed Variety or Vaudeville acts. All of the couples that took part in the contests were good singers and dancers, and the winning of the championship at Madison Square Garden was a great help to them in getting bookings from all over the world because this American dance which originated among the colored people during slavery was a sensation all over the globe." [44]

"They all bet on their favorite after they had seen all of the contestants as they walked around the ballroom. Some of the contestants had served them in some capacity during the season. While the couples were waiting to come out and do their stuff, some heavy betting went on. The contest was a hot one because couples would be eliminated by the applause of the audience. In addition, the lures were the cake and big cash prizes for the winners." [45]

Tom Fletcher had the chance to teach Cakewalk dancing, and he recalled one of his best students. "I got the champion cake-walker of the world at that time, a fellow called Pickaninny Hill. Hill had been a prize-fighter working with Muldoon, the top wrestler of that period," and "I was lucky enough to get the runners-up in the last championship cakewalk contest at Madison Square Garden that season along with Hill and the next day the newspapers described the affair as a great battle and a great party." [46]

Active during these years, Fletcher recalled, "[a]ll of the big colored shows featured the Cakewalk; the Black Patti Troubadours, Sam T. Jack Creole Company, Williams and Walker Company, *South Before the War* company, and all the big colored minstrel companies." "From then on, nearly every colored show, minstrels and all, put women in the cast. This made possible all sorts of improvisations in the Walk, and the original was soon changed into a grotesque dance. Furthermore, with women traveling with the companies, each couple began to work out its own original routines. A number of the men married their partners while traveling in the same companies." Another company, Henderson Smith's Creole Company, left this funny note about their travels in 1891: "We close our show with a funny afterpiece entitled, 'Don't you dance, if you do you will bust your religion,' by James Waco." At this point, we need to overview these various performing troupes.[47] One of the main shows to start around these years, taking a format close to the minstrel shows while also departing from it, was the Black Patti Troubadours.

As we have seen, some classical singing was also a regular part of the extension of minstrel shows. As a matter of fact, they often included a short operatic piece toward the end of the spectacle. Maybe the most famous opera singer of her time was Matilda Sissieretta Joyner Jones, known under the stage name Black Patti. She was born in Virginia in the late 1860s, but she started her stage career on the East Coast in the mid-1880s before reaching New York City in 1888. She quickly rose to fame and by 1892 was singing for the president and made a remarkable presentation at Madison Square Garden. She recalled, "I woke up famous after singing at the Garden and didn't know it." [50]

This show at Madison Square Garden was entitled the *Jubilee Spectacle and Cakewalk*. It included a Cakewalk contest, the Alabama Quartet backed by 400 singers, and a double banjo quintet. The Cakewalk dance was described as a "duple-time dance with simple syncopation." Some of the most outstanding cake walkers were present: Blackburn, already named by Fletcher, Snow and Shudder, Luke Pully, and Dandy Jim. The spectacle exhibited a "Southern shuffle executed by three colored damsels" and a fake fight by men in gloves. Only after this fancy list came Jones. Her fame granted her an invitation to the Chicago World's Fair of 1893, but in the end, complications prevented her from going. In 1896, she formed her private touring troupe.[51]

The Black Patti Troubadours crystallized the minstrel shows as a vehicle for the next generation of performers. The repertoire sung by Jones and her acolytes predates the era of the blues divas in the following sense: the show included a similar variety of performers that we will find under the tutelage of the blues divas, but it also constantly presented the singers at the crossroad of classical and popular singing. When the classical component of these singers' repertoire partly faded away, the term coined for these performers was 'coon shouters.' The word 'coon' clearly comes from the popularity of coon songs in the 1890s, as we have seen with Ernest Hogan's 'All Coons Look Alike to Me,' while 'shouters' will remain a descriptive artifact for the blues shouters well into the 20th century. Most of the early blues divas were first labeled 'coon shouters.' The blues also bore the name of 'folk's opera.' [52]

During the 1896-97 seasons of the Black Patti Troubadours, Jones toured with Bob Cole and his wife, the 'grotesque' or comic dancer Stella Wiley, acrobats Goggin and Davis, protean artist Tom Brown who had performed with Billy McClain earlier in his career, and Marguerite Las Oros the Cuban nightingale. The acrobatic team of the Fredricks was also doing pyramid constructions. Jones was in the operatic part of the show, a standard at the time commonly named the Operatic Kaleidoscope. Part of the Troubadours included the show *Oriental America*, similar to the Octoroons shows, which ended with 40 minutes of comical Opera. The Black Patti Troubadours were still close to minstrelsy with three parts; first came the humorous skits and dances, second, came the olio section with a variety of artists, but the third type was different with the Operatic Kaleidoscope. The Troubadours were a major institution during those years. They promoted the names of Bob Cole, George Walker, Bert Williams, Aida Overton Walker, Ernest Hogan, Will Marion Cook, J. Rosamond Johnson, Ida Forsyne, Jolly John Larkins, J. Ed. Green, Homer Tutt, S. Tutt Whitney, and Abbie Mitchell. Many of them would become central figures of African American entertainment. In the 1897 season Jones' troupe performed a song that already referred to the blues: 'Oh Susie' (Dis Coon Has Got the Blues).[53-58]

Whereas Jones was the star, the Cakewalk was the pinnacle of the evening. However, it was not the only dancing presented on stage. The opening part had a Honolulu dance, the olio had a Rag-Time Buck Dance and the trapeze team of The Watt's Coon Eccentric, and the show finished with The Grand Cakewalk and Ebony Ecstasies. The Black Patti Troubadours' main coon shouter was Mattie Phillips, from North Carolina, who sang 'Mr. Johnson Turn Me Loose,' and "set the audience wild, and her idea of the poetry of motion in the cake walk is wonderful to behold," said a critic. She was good enough to win herself a place in the olio in Philadelphia, where, with John Bailey, she introduced the 'rag-time shadow dance.' By 1902, Mattie Phillips was with the New Orleans Minstrels.[59-62]

For *At Jolly Cooney Island* in 1898, the show included Ernest Hogan, Tom Logan, Mattie Phillips, and Alice Mackey. Gus Hall and a Chorus sang 'Hot Time in the Old Town Tonight,' the Meredith Sisters did a 'Japanese Song and Dance' act, and the whole company laid down a buck dance. Hogan sang 'Enjoy Yourselves' with a chorus, Mattie Phillips offered 'Mr. Johnson Turn Me Loose,' and, finally, the show had the Grand Cakewalk during The Grand Kaleidoscope with opera songs. The troupe might have included more dances since Irving Jones, composer of the Pas Mas La and dancer himself, was in the Troubadours in 1900 and 1901, when critics congratulated him for being the "best interpreter of the modern ragtime ballad and one of the most accomplished composers of songs of that class." [63]

Tom Logan appeared in Bobby Kemp's Comedy Four in 1905, where Kemp danced while Logan helped with the comedy. Logan also joined the Smart Set in the following years. Alice Mackey performed with Williams and Walker.[64]

The Black Patti Troubadours also promoted Cakewalk contests on Saturday nights at Coney Island. Ida Forsyne, who worked with them between 1898 and 1902, also performed in small clubs. "It was all song-and-dance then–you'd sing a verse, then a chorus, and then dance a chorus you'd have to yell your songs in those crowded clubs. I was like a coon shouter until my voice gave out, and I used to have a wonderful alto." [65-66]

About the troubadours, she explained, "[w]e had a cakewalking contest every performance, and my partner and I won it seven nights straight in a row." She precised the "Cakewalk is something they had in the Civil War, the man who owned these people, every once in a while he'd get them out and have a party and tell them to do the Cakewalk. My mother was one [of the] people doing that cakewalk business." She added, "[e]verybody could prance a bit and smile," "raise your hand, look graceful." In particular, "smile was very important in my days." [67-68]

Ida Forsyne started dancing as a kid in Chicago, where she was born in 1883. Her mother was dubious of her skills at first, "[s]he didn't think I could dance, but I was picking up pennies dancing in front of the candy store when I was ten." "I was dancing all around the street all the time; I begged, and they asked me to dance." She was finally asked to participate in cake walking presentations, but at the time, "I didn't know nothing about the Cakewalk." It ended up being similar to what she did in the streets. She also learned some steps from Willie Mason, who played piano in a saloon over which the Forsynes lived. With a little boy, she danced in various events and clubs, and finally, she said, "I did the Cakewalk with a little boy at the Chicago World Fair" when she was nine years old, which helped her get even more gigs. "We did the Cakewalk every day" at social dances and other events. At that time, she claimed most people knew how to do it: "[i]t was so natural for blacks to do the Cakewalk, they liked to prance, the rear back, you know." She traveled in The Black Bostonian troupe, doing buck dance, which she explained was Legomania and eccentric dancing. Then, Tom Fletcher, who described her as "one of the clever girls from the early days," remembered she performed in Uncle Tom's show before joining the Black Patti Troubadours. Ida Forsyne toured Russia decades later with Sam Wooding's band and was labeled the "cake walking toast of Russia." [69-75]

Dancer Willie Glenn recalled the popularity of these Cakewalk contests, "[t]hey also had cakewalk competitions at Coney Island on Saturday nights and paid couples six dollars if you entered." It was advantageous, "[w]hen one of us dancers was out of work, we'd get a girl and go down there and pick up a little cash." Eddie Rector is another dancer who developed his Cakewalk at Coney Island.[76-77]

The minstrel and operatic traditions were not the only influences on ragtime shows of the 1890s. The exotic creoles captured the public's imagination, and promoters inevitably used it to their advantage.

Based on an idea by Sam Lucas, Sam T. Jack's *Creole Show* contained Sam and his wife, Fred Piper, Billy Jackson, and others. In the *Indianapolis Freeman* in 1890, a critic described the show at the London Theater in New York. First, he confirmed the promises offered by the title since the "show commenced with a very pretty first part, attractive groupings of shapely femininity," and he proceeded to give more details about the performers. "Florence Brisco was the first conversationalist; Florence Hines, the greatest living female song and dance artist, second and Mrs. Sam Lucas third. The olio sketches were very fine and called for numerous encores." The show ended with the burlesque *The Beauty of the Nile, or Doomed by Fire*, written by William H. Waits. In 1891, the show included Irving Jones, the song and dance artist who later wrote the Pas Ma La. Florence Hines did a male impersonation, and "[t]he prize dancing by Burrell Hawkins, Irving Jones, Burt Grant, Wesley Norris and Miles, Marie Valerie, Stacciona and Stabolo, with George Weston as banjo accompanist, was a feature that elicited much applause." The prize dance was most likely the Cakewalk. It also included May Bohee, daughter of one of the Bohee Brothers.[78-79]

The Bohee Brothers were the banjo playing and buck dancing duo of James Douglass, born in 1844, and George, born in 1856. They were from New Brunswick, Canada, but they grew up in Boston. They had their Bohee Brothers Minstrels, including James Bland, but they also worked for Callender's Georgia Minstrels and others. They moved to England, where they were popular in London in the 1880s and even made recordings in the 1890s. Apart from their own compositions, they played popular songs, did the Cakewalk, and sang anti-slavery protest songs.[80]

Silas Seth Weeks also recorded in Europe at the turn of the century. Born in 1868, in Vermont, Illinois, Weeks was at ease with many instruments like the guitar and the banjo, but made a point in raising the mandolin to higher standards as a solo instrument. He played in various guitar and mandolin groups and toured cities like Philadelphia, New York, Boston, and Montreal. His recordings were classical-oriented, but his long list of compositions includes polkas, gavottes (he recorded his 'Laburnum Gavotte'), waltzes, schottisches, a 'Fantastic Dance,' and his 'Rang Tang Dance.' He also wrote a Cakewalk, a dance for which a postcard from Europe presented him with his wife Eleanor Jones Weeks.[81]

Back to the exotic shows, an unimpressed critic wrote about the Creole Show in 1892; "singing and dancing characterizes the ability of Jack's present company of performers. The comedians are not above the average. The jokes are all stale and are heard every day by our street gamins and the canaille of the slums." Still, "[i]mprovement on Florence Hines' part is out of the question. Marie Valerie's wing-dancing is good and her skirt-dance is alright as far as the skirt is concerned. Dora Painter's wing-dancing is equally as good as that of Marie Valerie. Rhoda May Brooks is traveling undoubtedly on her good looks, conversational ability and Venus-like form." Finally, "[t]hey have huge feet to show in the challenge dancing contest, however." Later that year, we learned that "Billy Farrell, of Sam T. Jack's Creole Co., has a new specialty, which was put on for the first time in Baltimore. He calls it the leg laying dance." This could be some Legomania, confirming Ida Forsyne's recalling of the dance around that time.[82-83]

The following year, "[s]ix women from Honolulu, dancing what manager Jack styles the Hullu-Hullu gavotte, are this week added to the drawing powers of his

Creole Burlesquers." Jones was probably taking some time off, possibly to promote his Pas Ma La since a critic wrote that "Irving Jones rejoined Sam T. Jack's Creole Co. He is making a success with his new song, entitled 'The Parsamala Dance.'" Another critic wrote, "Irving Jones, in a single comedy act, raised much laughter. His turn is followed by another march and a gavotte. Smith and Johnson, in banjo songs and dances, are next, and 'Aunt Jane's Wooden Wedding,' incidental to which the dancing contest is introduced, concludes the show." The critic added that the "other stellar attractions are Irving Jones, in his Posmala Dance; the Mallory Bros., in their mandolin songs and dances and musical melange." The Mallory Brothers also performed in the Mahara Minstrels around the same time.[84-86]

Other historic performers joined the troupe around these years. Charles E. Johnson and Bob Cole, who had an act called *Colored Aristocracy* in the show, defeated 15 other buck dancers in Boston in 1893. Johnson recalled, "I just picked up dancin' on my own," precising, "[n]ever had a teacher. I was just a kid in my teens -shinin' shoes at the old Nicollet House in Minneapolis- when I started to work out soft shoe steps and the old buck and wing." Charles Johnson and his wife, Dora Dean, were doing a "grotesque song and dance" in 1894.[87-89]

In the same year, the troupe was again attempting to popularize a new dance. An appreciative critic wrote that the good dancers were "securing perfect freedom of movement. In this connection, Mr. Isham, among other dances, will introduce 'The Moonlight Minuet,' with an efficient corps de ballet, and all the mechanical and scenic effects calculated to insure success. 'The Moonlight Minuet,' which has never been presented on any stage, is a dance of joy, supposed to celebrate the close of the wet season in the tropical or equatorial latitude, in which the natives are said to indulge with an abandon of which the average terpsichorean artist is seldom capable, and yet with a grace that is entrancing. This dance, for which the surroundings of the new first part are peculiarly adapted, Mr. Isham believes will take its place among the sensational terpsichorean diversions of the day." We saw that some Caribbean dances probably reached Congo Square in New Orleans, even if in modified forms. The company voluntarily introduced a tropical dance to the stage in this case.[90]

In 1895 they made another attempt to popularize a dance, as pointed out in newspapers: "Among the new features recently added to this company is a novel dance, entitled 'La Danse Electrique,' in which the native belles, attired in rich and fascinating costumes, disport themselves in 'Under the Mistletoe Bough.'" In 1897, it included specialties Black Carl the Creole Mahatma, George Wilson, the Golden Gate Quartette with 'Washday on the Levee,' and Hypolite, a West Indian musical prodigy. The show closed with a skit called *The Soiree*, which probably included more dancing. Jim Grundy and Mundy, the grotesque dancers in the cast, were well-known dancers of the time.[91-92]

Around that time, a list of performers in the troupe was published; Belle Davis, Tom McIntosh and wife, Bole and Smart, Billy Johnson, Harry Singleton and wife, Sadie Jerry, Viola Jones, Marie Roberts, Stella Wiley, Kitty Brown, Mattie

Wilkes, Nellie Williams, Merrill Hursh, Maggie Brooks, Annie Ross, Rose Harper, Annie Smith, Annette D'Yone, and Alicia Favette. Some of these continued to appear in other shows in the following years.[93]

John W. Isham, who departed from the Creole Show after a dispute with Sam T. Jack, created the *Creole Opera*, then the *Octoroons*, in 1895. It cast Pete Hampton, Smart and Williams, the Hyers Sisters, Joe Britton, Marion Henry, and others. The opening musical skit, *7-11-77*, was written by Bob Cole, and in the olio, Billy Miller did a comic monologue and songs. Other important names were Belle Davis, Alberta Ormes, 30 clever singers and dancers, and the Brittons, "grotesque and comedy dancers." Joe and Saddie, the Brittons, a famous husband and wife team during the 1900s, were comedians, singers, champion buck-and-wing dancers, and comedy dancers. As noted by the critics, "the nimble footed Joe is a perfect spasm of terpsichorean gyrations from the time he comes on until he goes off." The Cakewalk duo of Charles Johnson and Dora Dean even complained they were copying their style.[94-95]

The Brittons were hired to play the *Follies Bergères* in Paris for 3 months in 1904, but seemingly stayed for 3 years and were popular again at their return in America; "[b]oth are classy eccentric dancers and singers." As a team, they had "the liveliest of dancing acts entitled 'How's That?,'" and "some of the finest dancing on the vaudeville stage." Even if they were a "dancing phenomenon" and Sadie was offered many diamonds, a critic wrote Joe would do better off without her. Others wrote they "are nimble dancers and Mr. Britton is the cleverest eccentric and novelty dancer seen here in many months," he is "doing great stunt with his feet." Elsewhere, he was labeled the "master of the art of fancy steps." They were still active in 1914.[96-103]

In *7-11-77*, Belle Davis and Marion Henry did comedy sketches. It included the act 'The Booking Agency' by William English and the novelty finale 'Thirty Minutes around the Opera.' Julius 'Jube' Johnson was also in the troupe; his name might refer to the Juba dance.[104-105]

Another critic pointed to different performances with the act 'The Twentieth Century Swells,' with electrical effects, a piece entitled 'The Dago and the Monkeys' where Tom Brown, Shortly May, and Ed Furber did "antics and danced well," and the "Spanish Serenade and Ballet' acts were thoroughly novel." The singing and dancing troupe of the Mallory Brothers also got more elaborate. Mazie Brooks, a harpist, married Ed Mallory, and Grace Halliday, violinist and singer who studied in New Orleans under Nickerson, the same who taught Jelly Roll Morton, married Frank Mallory. Both spouses joined the Mallory act. The Mallory Bros., with Mazie Books and Grace Halliday, were probably cake walkers in 1902 under the name of Oriole Trio: "[t]hey are good singers and lively dancers, but their principal charm is their inherent Southern power to conjure melody. The harp, piano, staff, hand and chime bells are played with telling effect, popular airs succeeding popular selections and operatic medleys." In addition, "their imitation of a colored brass band, in which everyone is leader, and depiction of a nocturnal raid upon a chicken coop by darkies is a gem of pantomime and musical comedy." [106-107]

Other members of the *Octoroons* included Florence Hines, still doing male impersonations, Bob Cole and Stella Wiley, duettists introducing new dance specialties, Irving Jones and his wife, and Goggin and Davis singing medleys and marches. The Southern Sunset finale had buck and wing and the Cakewalk. Another source named the 'Cakewalk Jubilee' as a finale. [108-109]

Isham's next enterprise was *Oriental America* in 1896-1897. It consisted of the finest talent available, including Sidney Woodward, a promising J. Rosamond Johnson, William C. Elkins, Pearl and Maggie Scott, and Inez Clough, who started in this show and later won fame as a member of the Lafayette Players Stock Company. The original cast also had Tom Brown, Harry Fiddler, Ruby Shelton, Billy and Jennie Eldridge, Stout Pane, Ed Wynn, Jesse Shipp, Jim Burns, Mattie Wilkes, the Meredith Sisters, who also toured with the Black Patti Troubadours with their Japanese act, Lottie Carrie, and others. It was the first show of this type to open on Broadway at Palmer's Theatre. The show was considered to be in good taste; it included the bridal chorus sextette from Lucia di Lammermoor in which all the stars appeared. Some of the material was used a few years later in the Troubadours: "Among the many features of the great show were a Japanese dance, cleverly rendered by Fanny Rutledge, Pearl Meredith, Alice Mackey, and Carrie Meredith, who sang and danced equally well and were prominent in all the ensemble scenes of the performance. A quartet of cycling girls in bloomers and twentieth-century maids, the maids of the Oriental Hussars, led by Miss Belle Davis, as well as the hunting scene and opening chorus from the Bells of Cornville." Bob Cole and Billy Johnson wrote some of the sketches that ended up in another show called *A Trip to Coontown*. [110-112]

In 1897 a reviewer detailed that in the olio, "Mr. and Mrs. Tom McIntosh are easily the leaders. Both have an intelligent idea of low comedy, and their act is full of new and original humor. Harry Fiddler, an excellent character mimic, is amusing, and Sam Lucas is giving a clever monologue. Others who appear on the bill are Billy Jackson, comedian, the 'Twentieth Century Swells,' Bethel and Jones in a character sketch, and the Spanish Serenaders." James Weldon Johnson, on his side, noticed the pretty chorus girls, organized just as *The Octoroons* were. [113-114]

Another early example of a well-received show with prominent casting organized by Al G. Fields in 1896 took place at Ambrose Park, South Brooklyn. Ambrose Park previously saw the Buffalo Bill Cody Show in 1895, including a whole 'Negro village' with cabins, chickens, and 500 African American performers acting, dancing, and singing songs like 'Roll, Jordan, Roll,' and 'Carry Me Back to Old Virginia.' The show ended with a buck-and-wing contest until exhaustion. Tom Fletcher again explained, "[t]he site chosen for the production was Ambon Park in Brooklyn, NY. The park was transformed into the likeness of a southern plantation. Cotton bushes with buds blossoming were transplanted. Bales of cotton were brought in and a cotton gin in working order set up. Poultry and livestock were brought in and real cabins built, a large part of the company using these cabins as living quarters for

66

the season. This entire layout provided atmosphere through which the audiences would roam at random before the show itself started. Fifteen minutes before show time, a signal would be given and the crowds would find their seats in the huge outdoor amphitheater which was covered by canvas." Also at Ambrose Park, George Wilson performed some buck-and-wing dancing in a show displaying "Negro racers, hurdle riders, gladiators, athletes, banjoists, specialists, wing and buck dancers and a perfect presentation of the Old Plantation Darkey." Early mentions of buck dancers were frequent in the 1890s. For a show in New York, "Tom Jefferson, Sloan Edwards and Jack Cook, singers, dancers and comedians . . . Joseph McCree, old-time colored jubilee singer, banjoist, and buck and wing dancer." [115-118]

For the spectacle, "the house was perfumed with jassimine by mechanical contrivance. The trees moved as if in a gentle breeze, and the perfume was seemingly wafting from the trees as the curtain went up." Comedian John Rucker sang 'Ringing the Old Village Bells,' and was encored, while "the Magnolia Quartet sang very nicely, and the Charleston Shouters, at the conclusion of the first part, made a hit, especially McIntosh. It is a new style of stage work and went big, the old camp meeting scene arousing the audience to a high pitch." Prof. Simpson opened the olio with a trombone solo, and Harry Fiddler "did a turn of very good imitations, his impersonation of Chinese character being the best." During the skit 'The Phantom Patrol,' the "buck and wing dancing was one of the big hits," and the "watermelon scene was funny enough to make an Indian laugh." [119]

The 1896 show, *Darkest America*, depicted the race history from plantation life to urban settings where the show itself took place. A critic described the cast as "bright and wholesome fun and their singing, dancing and sketch work is strictly up-to-date." Of national fame, Sam Lucas led the cast while his new wife Florence Hines rendered songs on violin and cornet in addition to singing a male impersonation. The crowd applauded dancer and actor James Crosby for his dancing and singing act. Billy McClain, Peter Hampton, and Billy Johnson, all three famous by then, also participated. Professor Henderson Smith's military band provided the music, and the show kept a spot for the Golden Gate Quartet. Another comedian and dancer in the show was George Titchner.

A reviewer in 1897 wrote that "the corn husking scenes in the barn, the massing singing and the wild antics of the dance in perfect time with the music was a perfect reproduction of the actions of the people they represented both on festival occasions and in a measure at Sunday wood's meetings." Another one spotted several new features to the scene 'The Barbers' Picnic' by the McCarver Brothers, "making it the strongest dancing act before the public" while Billy Jackson, Harry Fiddler, Billy Caldwell, and John Rucker's end work continued to please the public. The McCarver Brothers also had an act in the show called 'Georgia Cracker Jacks.' A picture of the cast doing the Cakewalk also exists. As Tom Fletcher said, all these shows used the Cakewalk. [120-121]

The widespread publication of ragtime music in the 1890s led to various titular Cakewalks presenting the dance on their covers. In 1877, we can already find 'Walking for Dat Cake' by Harrigan and Hart, where the dance seems to happen in a rural house with dancers balancing plates on their heads. The song was the highlight of the Mulliguard Guard show in 1877. On the cover of 'Dancing on the Kitchen Floor,' a Cakewalk song by James A. Bland, we can see dancers high kicking in the air. For 'Old Time Cake Walk' (1897), the covers showed a barn dance with rural cake walkers moving to the music of the banjo and an accordion. Ben Harney's 'Cakewalk in the Sky' (1899) mentioned the harps as a musical instrument to back the Cakewalk. The sheet music cover shows a rural environment with a woman playing the harp in the background. 'Loquatias Moll' (1900) presents imagery of rural cake walking with loose wrists, giving a comical effect. 'Hot Off the Griddle' (1915) shows a banjo player, a bone player, and a couple dancing. 'Jolly Pickaninnies' was described as a Schottische.[122]

Indeed, back to our previous dance, there is a reference in 1901 to a Pas Ma La Cakewalk in Tom Cabin's Show. The Rag Ma La was also mentioned in the same article. 'My Honolulu Baby' by Lee Johnson lets us know that the Honolulu Pas Ma La seems to be another term for Cakewalking; there are mentions of a prize at the end and some gliding and cutting the pigeon wing.[123]

The Cakewalk and ragtime dances, such as the Pas Ma La and others, probably evolved simultaneously. These dances often found their roots in rural areas and were also adapted to urban contexts. Their representation and descriptions in sheet music testify to their interrelations. Composer Ben Harney, author of 'Cakewalk in the Sky,' said that ragtime was synonymous with 'Negro Dance Time.' An impressed witness recalled Harney as a performer, that "Ben managed to sit at the piano with a cane in one hand or the other and did a sort of tap dance with one or both feet and the cane." The cover of 'His Ragtime Walk Won the Prize' showed a fancy couple cake walking in 1899, and 'A Hot Old Time in Ragtown' both explicitly link Cakewalks to ragtime music while still representing Cakewalk dancers. The song 'A Ragtime Masquerade,' in 1899, is described as a Cakewalk march and two-step. Rupert Hugues added that "Negros call their clog dancing 'ragging' and the dance a 'rag' (The dance is largely shuffling)." He added, "[t]he dance is a sort of frenzy with frequent yelps of delight from the dancer and the spectators, and accompanied by the latter with banjo-strumming and clapping of hands and stamping of feet. The banjo figuration is very noticeable in the rag music and the division of one of the beats into two short notes is perhaps traceable to the hand-clapping." Such dancing most likely appears on the cover of the sheet music of 'Uncle Jasper Jubilee' (a characteristic Cakewalk) and 'A Warmin'-Up in Dixie' (Cakewalk). An article from 1901, 'The Origin of Ragtime,' explains that the name came from a piece of rag cloth exhibited to inform a dance was happening and that the shake raggers' style became popular as ragtime dance. The evolution from the plantation dance seemed rather obvious to Pugh, who insisted that "ragtime dances had evolved from the cakewalk's high struts to a spate of quick two-steps," even if it was mostly an urban expression.[124-126]

The transition from rural to urban fancy dance is easily noticed in the sheet musical at the end of the 1890s. Despite some caricatural traits, there is a genuine intention to present the dancers of Cakewalks and 'characteristic marches' as fancy. Some visual representations of this fancier tradition have survived. A wood engraving of 1870 by William Ludlow Sheppard entitled 'The Cake Walk' shows three ladies parading the dance in front of an audience. Comparing the audience's clothing with that of the elegant dancing ladies shows that costume could be an important part of the dance's status. In 1889, a drawing published in an article by T. L. Robinson showed 'Walking for the Cake' with a dozen couples parading elegantly while the judges watched. A band, consisting of a fiddle and a cornet, provided the music.[127]

The covers of 'Hannah's Promenade' (1897), 'Liza Skinner the Southerner' (1899), 'Black Cinderella' (1900), and 'Audacious Arabella' all presented a solo fancy lady dancing while 'Prancin' Jimmy' (1899) presents a man. 'Eli Green's Cakewalk'(1898), 'Jasper Jenkins' (1898), 'An Old Virginia Cakewalk' (1899), 'Walkin on the Rainbow Road' (1899), 'Looney Coons' (1900), and 'Huckleberry Finn Cakewalk' (1900) all depict elegant couples dancing. They became more numerous on 'A Jolly South Carolina Cakewalk' (1899), 'Whistlin' Rufus' (also with fancy guitarist, 1899) 'Keep Movin'' and 'Colored Aristocracy Cakewalk' (1899). On 'Miss Cinda's Walk,' the fancy couples are backed by the banjo, the flute, and the violin. 'At a Georgia Camp Meeting' (1902), portrays the well-dressed partners in a rural context, while 'Aunt Minervy Anns' (1902) showed them in a dance hall. The popularity of the dance and related ballroom contests and stage productions led to the importance of fancy clothes related to the dance performance. Actress Sul Te Wan remembered she had to dress well when she met movie director D. W. Griffith, and she did so with one important dress. "I only had one dress that I used to do the cakewalk in way back in my young days when I used to cakewalk on the boats from Cincinnati, Ohio to Louisville, Kentucky." [128]

The proposition to link the Cakewalk to respectable standards was evident with the Black Patti Troubadours, but also with Johnson's Operatic Cake Walkers Company which included The Crosbys, Vida Devine, and Webster Williams; Addie May Scott, Percy Gudger; The Pettys—Billy and Betty; Arthur Dunnigan and Trixie Ford, and Harry Crosby in 1902.[129]

One of the most elegant Cakewalk teams was Billy and Willie Farrell, winners of the Richard K. Fox Championship Cakewalk Medals, who were seemingly very good and went to Europe and spread the dance around. The most famous cake walker couple, though, consisted of Johnson and Dean. Charles E. Johnson started on stage at Brown's Theater in Minneapolis in 1889 during an amateur show, before joining the Sam T. Jack Creole Company around 1891 or 1893, where Johnson sang and played the banjo. Dancer Thaddeus Drayton said of him, "Charlie Johnson was one of nature's noblemen." Among the chorus dancers was the beautiful Dora Dean Babbige, whom he married in 1893. Dora Dean was born in Covington, Kentucky, around 1872. George L. Moxley, an African American performer, often passing for white, and who later was Mr. Interlocutor in the Mahara Minstrel with W.C. Handy, recalled her with the Sam Lucas company as "the first woman to do the cakewalk." Many noticed her beauty, like Tom Fletcher, who wrote she was "one of the country's most beautiful colored girls." Ragtime pianist Joe Jordan also had kind words for her: "She was a strutter and a beautiful something to look at." "When she walked in, the room caught on fire." Dancer Rufus Greenlee added that "Miss Dean had a fabulous personality." "Dora was just as clever a dancer as she was beautiful, and this made the team a great couple." They were featured in many theatrical companies around the country and were at all society events.[130-137]

After participating in the Chicago World's Fair, the newspapers crowned them as King and Queen of colored Aristocracy. Johnson's mother, born in slavery, would have been proud of the title since it was a piece of advice he clearly remembered from his mother, "[b]e a gentleman." The duo Johnson and Dean introduced the Cakewalk to New York in 1891 or 1895. After confirming Johnson's early days as a dancer in various styles, Tom Fletcher wrote, "[t]he old 'chalk-line walk' was revived with fancy steps by Charlie Johnson, a clever eccentric dancer, who later married Miss Dora Dean, also a dancer." [138-140]

"Way back in those first days of our team," Johnson said, "we decided the one thing that would make our act different was 'class.' None of that 'Uncle Tom' humour for us!" The theme song for their act was 'Georgia Camp Meeting.' [141]

"Johnson and Dean, like all colored performers, were always striving to improve, and they were the first to use the Flicker Kinetoscope, a spotlight with a glass built on the inside and a handle on the outside. At a given cue the stage lights would be turned off and the house lights dimmed. Charley Johnson, dressed in a black Prince Albert or full dress suit, with white gloves and white spats, and Dora, with a dark dress trimmed in white, would come on and go into their dance. The Kinetoscope would be turned on while they were dancing and when the spot-light hit them, the operator would turn the handle making the glass on the inside of the machine whirl, with the result that the couple on the stage looked like a crowd of hands and feet and nothing else." [142]

Their fame brought them to Europe, where they were well received. An article from 1912 portrayed Dora while she was still teaming with Johnson as the best African American singer-dancers. The description underlined her sense of aristocracy: "Her jewelry with this costume included a 200-guinea set of diamond earrings, a 500-guinea diamond sunburst necklace and a 300-guinea diamond sunburst worn over the breasts." Coming back from Europe, Dora was tired of performing. She opened a fashion shop with her friend Mattie Wilkes, Ernest Hogan's wife, whereas "Charley Johnson, just like an old firehorse, didn't want a vacation from the stage, so when he met his old friend and fellow trouper, Irving Jones, who had a big reputation in America and Europe, the two joined up as a team. Johnson, a great dancer, and Jones, a great comedian, made a very good team. Billed as 'Irving Jones and Charley Johnson, Two Cut-ups' their act scored quite a success." Irving Jones, again, was the composer of the 'Pas Ma La.' [143-144]

Cakewalks were first filmed around the time the team of Dean and Johnson reached their peak. In 1894, Joe Rastus, Denis Tolliver, and Walter Wilkins were in Lucy Daly's Pickaninny troupe in *The Passing Show* that had played at New York's Casino Roof Garden in 1894. The other eight dancers from their troupe did not appear on film. Filmed by Edison's assistant William K.L. Dickson, they moved irregularly, stomped, and fell but just kept on with the show. Their dancing, accompanied by harmonica playing, was frantic, and the film is one of the best dance testimonials of the time. In the documentation of the time, it was described as a jig, clog, and cakewalking.

We find another famous performer in James Grundy. He was born in Arkansas in 1861, and at the age of six, was with his brother Will in the Little Nugget Company, then in Dr. Fitzgibbon's Medicine Show, and then joined the show *The South Before the War*. His wife Susie was also a performer.

This show from 1891 featured other popular performers of the time—for instance, Ed Green, born in Indiana in 1872. Green showed early skills as a comedian and vocalist, toured with Madame Selika, and performed in clubs and churches. In 1892 he formed the Diamond Quartet with three other fellows; Ed. Hood, I. M. Smith, and La Force. They were hired for *The South Before the War* shows, where Green also had a role and directed a chorus. This quartet is not to be confused with The Four Black Diamonds, formed in San Francisco with H.M. Johnson, Walter Dixon, Norris Smith, and Eugene Abbott, who toured mostly in Europe presenting parody of Bavarian songs and dances. These diamonds also recorded a handful of titles in Europe, including 'That Dixie Rag,' 'On the Mississippi,' and 'If the Man in the Moon Were a Coon,' most likely related to the *Sun* newspaper's hoax about having found men on the moon.[145-146]

Jubilees in Tom's shows were so typical by the 1890s that a show promised no shouters, no 'slaves before the war,' and no jubilee in their presentations. Still, most productions had it all, like one by Jarrett and Palmer that included songs and dances from the antebellum years like 'Dan Tucker,' 'Nelly Bly,' 'Dandy Jim' and a camp shouter.[147-148]

In Topeka, Ohio, in 1892, the South Carolinian Jubilee Singers had a band that also played for a select dance evening the next day, and "[t]he Renix brothers, three in number and Mr. Parquette, we feel safe to say that they cannot be beat in playing the mandolin and guitar. Mr. Parquette has but few equals in acrobatic dancing and singing." [149]

In 1894, the show *Down in Dixie* had the Florida Quartette in a scene as cotton pickers, while *On the Mississippi*, a comedy about the machinations of the KKK, included electric fireflies, croaking frogs, Mardi Gras costumes, and so on.[150]

By the decade's end, the troupe of the McAdoo's Virginia Jubilee Singers continued the mixture of secular and religious. They presented songs and dances from the South, including Jerry Mills, and Joe Jalvan, an acrobatic singing comedian also in the McAbe's Minstrels and later the stage manager at the Pekin theater in Chicago. In 1898, "[i]n the Olio, Jerry Mills in 'Silence and Fun' went through a remarkable performance, every method of perambulation being adopted, except the correct one. His finale consisted of an exposition of high kicking. Jalvan introduced an entirely new juggling performance and "[t]he performance concluded with 'The Cake Walk,' in which the members of the Company advanced by pairs in a most graceful manner to a large cake placed on a table, the audience selecting the winners by acclamation. After considerable competition the prize was awarded to Jalvan and Miss Gibbons." [151-152]

In 1899, the McAdoo's had the song-and-dance team of Hen Wise and Kate Milton and renamed the troupe Georgia Minstrels and Alabama Cakewalkers.[153]

There was a management war between Curtis and McCadoo's troupe when traveling in Australia, which led to Mr. Curtis's Afro-American Minstrel Company being described in the newspapers in 1899: "The Kentucky Four did some exceedingly clever buck and wing dancing; and Siren Navarro, the lilliputian creole contortion danseuse, twisted and twirled in a risque and an alarming fashion. The performance concluded with the laughable Cake Walk in which the competition between the various couples was very keen." Ernest Hogan also participated in this troupe. He had fought with a white man at a theater in New Orleans, and as Tom Fletcher said he told him, stopped shaking out of fear only once in Australia.[154-155]

Leading another troupe in Australia at the same time, Horace Copeland wrote he "was one of the first colored clog dancers in America and a member of many of the leading minstrel companies. I was founder and principal comedian and dancer of Corbyn's Georgia Minstrels that left San Francisco" for Sydney. After collapsing, Curtis's troupe was stuck in Australia, and Hogan formed a new company. For his *Uncle Eph's Return* show, the "second part displayed the dancing talent of the company, and in the Kentucky Four" with Katie Carter, Muriel Ringold, Amon Davis, and Livers, brought"quite new effects in dancing being presented." [156-157]

As in the United States, the minstrel shows followed the tradition of presenting elements from spirituals on stage, sometimes related to dance. Still active in Australia, the "McAdoo's Minstrels put on a Georgia Camp Meeting—Introducing the American Rag-Ma-La-Dance by the Company," probably referring to the Pas-Ma-La dance craze from half a decade before. The troupe later did a "Honolulu Dance" and included star Billy McClain. McClain, at the time. was teamed up with Charles Walker.[158]

Charles Walker was married to Ida May. In 1900 they were known as America's Gold Medal Cake Walkers, and they ended their careers in Britain, where a newspaper clip told Charles Walker's late life story in London. "Behind this dancing in darkness there is hidden a story of amazing pluck and stoicism. Walker always danced. Even in the days when he was a pickaninny there was laughter in his feet. He danced as one who loves dancing. He had a genius for dancing. He made a reputation for dancing in two hemispheres. Then suddenly, when he was in Australia, in the heyday of his prosperity, all the light and, as it seemed to him, all the dancing of his

life were suddenly shut out. Atrophy of the optic nerve blinded him almost instantly."
The tragedy did not prevent him from traveling. "Soon after his arrival in England he
went to the Brixton Music Hall, and without any practice gave his usual turn. He
walked quite naturally to the stage by the side of his wife and danced elaborate coon
dances and cake walks without a mistake. The second part of the turn was with his
wife, and here again he accomplished the feat by dancing and singing and talking
humorous dialogue without any one in the audience knowing he was blind. His wife
helped him by saying occasionally under her breath, 'one step this way,' or 'not so far
back,' and also by lightly touching him to show him where she was." "He was able
to do it by knowing the position of every musical instrument in the orchestra. While
the orchestra was playing he felt safe, as he knew from the sounds of the musical
instruments exactly where he was. When the orchestra was silent he moved about as
little as possible." Bravely, "[a]s he got on the stage, he tapped the drop curtain with
his hand, and then boldly walked forward into darkness—smiling. And for nearly a
quarter of an hour he danced about the stage, and walked backward and forward and
laughed and sang—in darkness. It was only at the end of eighteen months that he told
the manager of a music hall he was blind." [159]

Billy McClain, for his part, joined the show *South Before the War*. It had
started in 1892, casting Dancing Charley, buck dancer Annie Scott, the Eclipse
Quartet with Albert E. Anderson, who, separately with his brothers Morris and York,
had formed song and dance teams in other minstrel shows. Over the years, the show
also used many half-religious singing groups like the Twilight and Buckingham
Quartette and the Standard that recorded many songs, including Sam Lucas's 'Every
day will Be Sunday.' After *South Before the War*, Sam T. Jack hired McClain for his
Creole company, where he met his future wife and vaudeville partner, Mamie Riley.
In vaudeville, he worked with many stars and originated the comedy routine of
hunting his shadow across the stage with a lamp. [160-161]

South Before the War also included the Cakewalk, and a buck-and-wing
contest, probably Grundy's specialty. In the following years, Grundy toured important
shows and led different troupes of actors in Memphis and Chicago. For the
'Blackville Society,' with Cakewalks and 'coon songs,' Grundy was on stage with
Lulu Coates, Ruby Grundy, Sue Grundy, Pick Grundy, and the team of Rastus and
Blanks. When Grundy was a clog dancer in the Watermelon Trust Company, a
reporter informed the reader he came from no dancing school; he was "fresh and hard
to beat." [162]

In the show, Sherman Coates was one of the members of the original
Golden Gate Quartet, with Frank Sutton, Arthur Coates, and Henry Winfred. In 1898,
after their performance, the "challenge of Coates and Annie Sutton for a cake walk
was accepted...by Peter Barnes and partner." The same year he sang with Mabel
Bohee in a show including singer and dancer Phyllis Price. For the Watermelon Trust,
Sherman Coates did the soft shoe. Gertie Miller was part of the Watermelon Trust
company in 1907 with the wives of Grundy and Coates. They "do some marvelous
as well as dangerous steps because of the position it places them in." The reporter

added that "in animation, in grace of pose and gesture, in all the sweet and eloquent infections of cultivated songsters and dancers, these actresses are invaluable." [163-165]

Anyhow, Grundy, a skillful buck dancer, went from the *South Before the War* to Sam T. Jack's Creole Show, where he met his future wife, Susie Grundy. It must have been around that time that circumstances brought him to dance the Cakewalk in front of Thomas Edison's camera in 1895, but the film was lost.[166]

In 1897, the Edison company made *Dancing Darkey Boy*, in which a little boy dances on a platform in front of a crowd, similar to the 'Dancing for Eels' tradition. Again, it shows some buck dancing, while the documentation indicates the Cakewalk.

More convincing cake-walking films were made in 1903 by the American Mutoscope & Biograph Company. In the first, described as 'Coon Cake Walk,' two couples and a single dancer strut, hold hats and canes and walk around dressed impeccably. In the second entitled Comedy Cake Walk, the formation is similar, but the dancing is caricatural; the dancers hop, kick and flap their bent knees.

There is also a beautiful cake walking scene from 1903 in Edward S. Porter's film *Uncle Tom's Cabin*, also a popular show at the time, as we have seen with Sam Lucas. The short film shows couples strutting around, and a lady holding an umbrella exhibits various dance moves. The film also shows buck dancing and square dancing with swinging partner motions. Cake walking, otherwise, appeared rarely on film.

Nevertheless, its presence on screen might have inspired the description of a Dean and Johnson performance in 1903, where Dora Dean was labeled as a coon shouter. "Their kinetoscope dance was a decided feature." As explained by Fletcher, this device was a novelty in their act, but it was also part of the cinematic experiments during these years.[167]

The increasing popularity of the dance in Northern urban centers inevitably led to it becoming the topic of some shows. In 1898, the classical violinist and ragtime composer Will Marion Cook collaborated with writer Paul Laurence Dunbar to write the operetta *Clorindy: The Origin of Cakewalk*.

Will Marion Cook was born in 1865 in Washington, D.C., and moved with his grandparents to Chattanooga 10 years later, where he caught on to African American folk melodies. After moving back with his mother to the capital, he started learning classical violin. Cumulating frustrations in the segregated classical world led him to stop giving classical concerts after a critic called him the best 'colored' violinist in the world; Cook thought his color should have been omitted. He toured with a small chamber orchestra and wrote *Scenes from the Opera of Uncle Tom's Cabin,* planned to be presented at the Chicago World's Fair in 1893 in collaboration with Black Patti. He dedicated some time to music writing and then concentrated on his *Clorindy* project.[168-169]

He struggled initially to find actors for the show, but got lucky when the increasingly popular comic Ernest Hogan volunteered for the show after hearing

Cook play the theme song in a restaurant. The show recounted the origin of the Cakewalk in Louisiana in the 1880s. Supposedly written in one night, it included Belle Davis, a singing, dancing, cake walking creole woman from Texas who had been in the Creole Show, the Octoroons, and *Oriental America*. The show opened at the Casino Roof Garden in New York and was an instant hit. Cook himself stated, "[m]y chorus sang like Russians, dancing meanwhile like Negroes, and cakewalking like angels, black angels." Satisfied with this sudden success, Cook got himself "gloriously drunk," drinking alcohol he mistook for water. Dunbar, on the contrary, was shocked to realize Hogan had washed away parts of the story and cut some lyrics from the songs to give it a stronger minstrel flavor.[170-173]

After its summer run, it became part of the show *Senegambian Carnival* for a tour during which Cook met Abbie Mitchell, a classically trained singer, and added her to the show. As the story goes, Mitchell was singing on a fire escape when someone heard her voice and recommended her to sing in the chorus of *Clorindy*. She went for an audition, sang classical songs, and Cook told her she could not sing a damn thing. Cook sat at the piano and played his compositions. She recalled, "'[t]hat's the kind of music you should sing,' he said. 'That's Negro music and you're ashamed of it!' I tried to defend myself by explaining that decent colored girls did not sing coon songs or ragtime, as it was then called." Mitchell was to end up years later in the films *Uncle Remus' First Visit to New York*, *Lime Kiln Club Field,* and *Junction 88,* although she is better known for being the first to record Gershwin's 'Summertime.' Belle Davis, on her hand, continued to perform during the next decade as Belle Davis and Her Crackerjacks in Southern Pastimes. She also toured Europe as a 'coon shouter,' ragtime singer and dancer. She married actor Henry Troy, and recorded the ragtime title 'Just Because She Made Dem Goo-Goo Eyes.'[174]

James Weldon Johnson was ecstatic about the show: "Cook was the first competent composer to take what was then known as rag-time and work it out in a musical way. His choruses and finales in Clorindy, complete novelties as they were, sung by a lusty chorus, were simply breath-taking. Broadway had something entirely new."[175]

Cook's next two shows did not equal the popularity of *Clorindy*. After the failure of *Casino Girl* with Dunbar, Cook did the one-act *Jes Lak White Fo'ks* that opened at the New York Winter Garden in 1900, casting Ernest Hogan, Irving Jones, and Abbie Mitchell.[176]

Irving Jones had continued to be active, mostly as a singer. In an 1899 show under Ernest Hogan, with Billy McClain, Lawrence Chenault, soubrette Luela Price, a Cakewalk contest, Tom Logan, Kattie Carter and Muriel Ringgold for singing and buck dancing contests. There was the Criterion Quartet, with Irving Jones, George Jones, William Jones, and Amon Davis. Jones also led the band.[177]

Jones was with Sadie Jones in the Black Patti Troubadours in 1900; she sang 'Rag Time Liza,' and he sang his 'All Birds Looks Like Chicken to Me.' The opening chorus was the Honolulu Dance, many artists danced throughout the show, Nellie Goff did a trombone solo, and it ended with the Cakewalk. He was in a trio with Sadie Jones and Bert Grant in 1900, probably the same Sadie with whom he performed in 1901 in Chicago, with Seymour and Dupré. The following year, still writing 'coon songs,' he took part in a show including the song and dance team of Ritter and Leavitt, in another one with Al and Mamie Anderson and ended up in 'The Cowboy and the Lady' including dancers Sherman and De Forest. He made a reputation for his singing and facial contortions, still noticed in 1909. There was a mention that his act with a performer named Blacks dissolved in 1910, and he seemed to still work with Sadie Jones and Bert Grant.[178-185]

Cook followed with *Uncle Eph's Christmas* in 1901, again with Ernest Hogan and Paul Dunbar. It also included Charles Hart, Louis Salisbury, Theo Pankey, Abbie Mitchell, Kid Frasier, dancer Ollie Burgoyne, Gertie Petterson, and Muriel Ringgold, amongst others.

The same year, *The Cannibal King* (1901) was a comic opera in two acts with lyrics by Bob Cole and Rosamond Johnson. It cast Bob Cole, Ernest Hogan, Billy Johnson, Theo Pankey, Lewis Salisbury, Abbie Mitchell, Mamie Grant, Anna Cook, Muriel Ringgold, Cecil Watts, Mollie Dill, Gertie Petterson, and Kid Frasier from his previous shows, the Alabama Comedy Four, "and a chorus of forty well-trained voices." Also in the show were Hen Wise and dancer Katie Milton, who toured as a team in 1902 with 'pickaninnies' Eugene King and Leo Bailey. During their tour, Milton was described as graceful. Wise and Milton made a well-received comeback in 1911 that included an Indian scene. In addition, the *Cannibal King* cast Coley Grant, who had performed in Kansas City with Tom Brown and Billy McClain in 1887 and would perform as late as 1927 in *Sons of Rest*. Finally, an Aida Walker participated, although it is unclear if it is Aida Overton Walker.[186]

In newspapers around the turn of the century, we can find the names of other performers who are not that well remembered otherwise but who are valuable in understanding the popularity and various appearances of the Cakewalk steps and the kind of shows that continued to include them in the first decade of the century. The *Florida Morning Tribune* in 1899 advertised Lucy Pethus as a renowned dancer, singer, and cakewalker performing at the Buckingham Theater Saloon. Lew Payton and Hattie Harris, known as grotesque cake walkers and comedians, got married on stage in 1900 at the Olympia in Houston, with music provided by Prof. R.J. Anderson's brass band to attract the crowds. On different occasions, Payton and Harris were labeled 'Georgia coon shouters,' or 'champion cakewalkers.' They were in Graham's Genuine Southern Specialty Company with the Wilsons (Jas. and Mable) (song, dance, sketch) and Cleo Desmond, a changing artist and possibly active in the 1910s as a dancer. The final skit was 'A Scene on a Haunted Camp Meeting Ground.' For another show with a quartet, there was a Honolulu Dance, and burlesque Cakewalk.[187-191]

In 1902, Mr. and Mrs. Walter, cake walkers, were in the African Concert Company. The same year, Billy B. Johnson, Will Reid, and future 'Jaz singer' Estelle Harris, who had just finished a burlesque version of *Foxy Quiller* and a 'military act' at the Tivoli Hall in Memphis, joined the *Johnson Operatic Cake Walkers and Museum*, the last part being rather a sideshow with a bearded woman and a snake charmer. In 1903, the Kemp Family show with Billy, his wife, and children, did 'Dancing by Aunt Monday and Uncle Joe,' 'Dancing on the Old Plantation,' 'Now We Will Have the Cake Walk,' 'Dancing by Mr. Kemp' and 'Dancing Over the Broom.' This last may relate to the older tradition depicted in *The Old Plantation* painting from the late 18th century. The Kemp family also included a variety of acts like 'How to Spell Chicken' and 'Banjo with Autoharp and Singing.' [192-194]

Charles Wright, known as C.W. Bebee in minstrel and medicine shows, was at the Olympic Theater in Galveston, Texas, and was described as doing "lightning cake walker and dummy dancer" with King and Simmons's Southern Black Troubadours. With the Proctor's Arkansas Minstrels, he was singing 'Chicken Can't Roost Too High for Me' in Alabama around 1905. The Rockwell's Sunny South Company in 1908 had 'Coons Prancing' to "Two-Step Rather than Waltz." In this case, we can understand that the term prancing, often used for the Cakewalk, also described some waltz dancing. The Colored Jubilee Singers was another touring troupe with 25 male and female singers, dancers, and cake walkers, as they appeared in Louisville. [195-197]

The most popular cake walkers after Johnson and Dean remained the pair of Bert Williams and George Walker. Williams was born in the Bahamas in 1874, but his family quickly moved to Florida and then California. By 1893, he was in the Martin and Selig's Mastodon Minstrels in San Francisco, where he met George Walker. Walker was born in Kansas in 1873 and performed as a child in minstrel and medicine shows. After forming a team, they got a chance to go to the Chicago World Fair as two natives in the Dahomean village. They probably had participated in some village dances since the Dahomey village displayed such shows. Performer George Moxley, who had "first met Williams and Walker in an upstairs 'Beer' theater in San Francisco," recalled, "[t]hey were singing and dancing between the tables. I did not know them, but we became acquainted." Their real success was going to be in New York. [198-200]

In honor of the queen of aristocracy, Bert Williams published his first composition 'Dora Dean: the Hottest Gal You Ever Seen' in 1896. In the lyrics, the famous dancer is described as the Louisiana queen, going to church on Sunday and keeping the house clean while beating everyone at cake walking: "way down in Louisiana, dat's where ole sister Hannah bakes the cracklin' bread upon the coal, with her daughter Dora Dean, who is my dearest queen. Oh I tell you she is a hump of gold, we all did feel so jolly, each one tried to cut the pigeon wing, when up jump'd Dora Dean, who said I am the queen, I can beat you up in a dance for anything, then they dance to the music in minor tone, and Dora walk'd with the cake." The version recorded in 1962 by ragtime pianists Joe Jordan, Eubie Blake, and Charles Thompson included a joke about playing in G flat and not being able to get to Dora's flat.

Both Williams and Walker were skilled cake walkers. Essie Whitman, part of the Whitman Sisters troupe, recalled Bert Williams, her neighbor as a kid: "He was the greatest strutter of them all." The aficionado of African American culture Carl van Vechten also described Williams's dancing enthusiastically: "How the fellow did prance in the cakewalk, throwing his chest and his buttocks out in opposite directions, until he resembled a pouter pigeon more than a human being." [201-202]

Dancer Walter Crumbley recalled, "George 'Bon Bon' Walker was the greatest of the strutters, and the way he promenaded and pranced was something to see." Singer Thomas 'Chappy' Chappell even went as far as to say, "Walker was the man who turned the Strut into the Cakewalk and made it famous." Dancer Ralph Cooper insisted: "But George Walker transformed the cakewalk into a high-style promenade. By rejecting the old, shuffling 'Yazuh boss' trend, he brought class top hat and tails to the cakewalk and made it a work of art." Their fame and social stance as cake walkers were such that when they heard Tom Fletcher was teaching it to white dancer William Kissam Vanderbilt, they challenged Vanderbilt to a dancing duel, which he never answered.[203-206]

Williams and Walker created the show *The Gold Bug* in 1896 for the Casino Theater in New York, which helped popularize the Cakewalk to a broader white audience. After the show, they took an engagement with Koster and Bial. "It was during this engagement that Williams and Walker made the Cakewalk not only popular, but fashionable. They were assisted by two girls; one of them, Stella Wiley, was the cleverest colored soubrette of the day. Cakewalk pictures posed by the quartet were reproduced in colors and widely distributed as advertisements by one of the big cigarette concerns. And the execution of the Cakewalk steps was taken up by society." [207-208]

These lines by James Weldon Johnson refer to the American Tobacco Company, who asked to photograph Williams and Walker for use in advertisements. They added two female dancers from the Black Batti Troubadours: Stella Wiley, Bob Cole's wife, and Aida Overton, who would add Walker to her name by marrying George. The trio of Henry Wise, Bob Cole, and Stella Wiley were described as "delsartean dancers" when working for the Troubadours, and Wiley was no stranger to the Cakewalk. The advertisements were so popular they were reproduced as lithographs and postcards. John Stark, Scott Joplin's publisher, even put the picture on the first edition of 'Maple Leaf Rag.' Joplin had brought a kid to dance to the tune for the publisher, which proved convincing.[209-210]

Initially, Will Marion Cook and Dunbar designed *Clorindy: the Origin of Cakewalk* for Williams and Walker, but, unfortunately, they were not available for the contract. As we have seen, when Abbie Mitchell joined the *Clorindy* troupe and Ernest Hogan left the cast, the show became the afterpiece to the *Senegambian Carnival*, which was Williams and Walker's second stage effort. A critic described the show as "a cakewalk monstrosity of a musical comedy," and was later renamed *A Lucky Coon*. In 1898 the show welcomed Lottie Thompson Williams's soon-to-be wife. She kept an important role in subsequent Williams and Walker shows. Anita

78

Bush, who also joined the chorus line for the troupe, recalled her mostly as a singer even if she appeared in some Cakewalk pictures. The show was also the basis of Cook's *The Policy Players*.[211-216]

The next show Williams and Walker produced in 1901, *Sons of Ham*, had a book co-written with Jesse A. Shipp, who had worked for *Oriental America* and *A Trip to Coontown*. Lyrics for the songs were by Alex Rogers, and the music again by Will Marion Cook. The principal cast included the two main couples with the support of Hattie McIntosh and Jesse A. Shipp. Critics noted acts related to their previous show: "There are but two specialties. One of these is a small Chinese bit by George Catlin, who makes up too white, and the Reese Brothers, who are assisted by Fred Douglass in an acrobatic and gun juggling specialty." Some singing came from Lloyd G. Gibbs, Alice Mackey, Anna Cook, and Pete Hampton. Charles Hart was also in the cast at some point.[217]

The show followed two students at Risk University (a pun on Fisk University), Williams and Walker, itinerants in Denver but mistaken for two twins coming back from abroad to claim an inherited fortune. It was revealed that the real twins had learned acrobatics, so the itinerants had to pretend to have that skill, which probably led to amusing scenes.[218]

Of interest were many songs from the show that were recorded on cylinders. Williams recorded the comical song 'Phrenologist Coon' as a doctor reading head bumps, for Victor records in 1901. In the science mocking trend, there was also 'Fortune Teller Coon,' which was dropped from the show the first year and recorded by Williams as 'Fortune Teller Man.' Williams also waxed the catchy African parody 'My Little Zulu Babe' (1901) backed by Walker doing some hollering, even if it was Walker singing the song during the show. Williams' song 'My Castle in the River Nile' was recorded by white 'coon song' specialist Arthur Collins, and The Deep River Boys recorded the song in 1946 for Pilotone in a peppy version.[219]

In the show, Walker also sang the dance-related 'The Leaders of the Ball' while Aida Overton sang 'Society,' and 'Hannah from Savannah,' considered the main hit from the show. It helped raise Aida Overton to star status. Harmonica champion Tom Lemonier, born in New York in 1870, wrote both 'Hannah from Savannah' and 'I Want to Be a Real Lady' for Overton Walker. Hal Johnson recorded the song, and Cousin Joe from New Orleans made a rock boogie version more than half a century later. Related was 'Hard Hearted Hannah' (The Vamp from Savannah), recorded by Marjorie Royer for Edison and later by others, including Ella Fitzgerald and Ray Charles.[220-221]

Critic Chicot, who saw a performance at the Bijou Theater, remarked on the increasing talent of Aida Overton, although she did not yet read the lines as well as Lottie Williams. The critic could not let the chorus line go unnoticed either, pointing in particular to the skin shades. "The chorus is lighter in tint than ever before. There is one girl with brown hair who used to be in the Isham forces, and several are almost white. A few of them are not bad looking, but there are some that are worse than straight blacks."

Confused by some fashion details, the critic also wrote, "[t]here is one girl who wears her hair straight on one side and curled on the other, who is utterly impossible, and there is one small black person who looks the chambermaid in a cheap hotel in a small Ohio town and will never look like anything else. She is too insignificant, she is funny to look at. The bold black chorus is a thing of the past apparently, and the change is not wholesome." The critic finished by turning to the other gender: "The male chorus is amusing. Some of the people have a knack of wearing clothes well, but others are at sea in evening dress, and do not look the part they are supposed to play. The singing is all good. They need more practice, and this will come when they have been out a little longer." This was especially true for a religious song.[222]

Florence Mills, a major artist of the Harlem Renaissance, got her first big show engagement at the age of eight at the Bijou Theatre in Washington when she appeared in a production of *The Sons of Ham*. She was billed as 'Baby Florence Mills, an Extra Added Attraction' and sang 'Miss Hannah from Savannah,' taught to her by Aida Overton Walker. Florence Mills recalled the event herself: "From the age of eight when I appeared in a production called *The Sons of Ham* it has just been one long fight for success. Always there was the bogy of my color barring the way. That I was able to win through it all was due to sheer determination to rise superior to prejudice." [223-224]

Again by Williams and Walker with a book co-written by Jesse A. Shipp, lyrics by Alex Rogers and Paul Laurence Dunbar, and music by Will Marion Cook, *In Dahomey* opened in 1902 at the New York Theater on Time Square. The next year it was popular in England, even enjoying a presentation at Buckingham Palace. It included the usual couples of Williams, Walker, and wives, and again the support of Jesse Shipp, Hattie McIntosh, and Peter Hampton. It also starred Abbie Mitchell and J. Leubrie Hill.[225]

In Dahomey was based on Cook's previous comic opera *The Cannibal King*. A famous comical scene starred a medicine man in Boston selling an elixir to turn colored folks white; a scene captured as a photo for posterity. Anita Bush seemed to say the scene came with a dance, although she placed it with the show *Abyssinia*, another Williams and Walker production. *In Dahomey* told the story of an unscrupulous businessman trying to convince another man in Florida to invest in lands in Africa. It was filled with pseudo-African references, waltzes, operatic singing, and Africanesque dances with drums. The inspiration probably dated back to the Dahomey village from the Chicago Fair of 1893, in which Williams and Walker were cast.[226-229]

Critic Sylvester Russell wrote about *In Dahomey* in 1902 and noted that improvements had been made in the first several months. "Much of the music of the original production has been wisely cut out. Will Marion Cook, technically speaking, is not a dealer in lyric harmony, and intonation, neither does his music have much of that breath of feeling that reaches the heart. His most classical selections are jerky, and everything he writes borders on a favorite set in minor chords whose mechanism has made his rag-time music famous." The new music was by Will Accooe, and, in general, the show was a success. Russell also wrote, "[g]irls will be girls and Aida Overton Walker is one girl fashioned after many who have become stars and made their fortunes. Her one short histrionic spasm of modern aristocracy is a little something to marvel at." He also praised Lizzie Harding, who replaced Alice Mackey for 'Dancing Sue.' We recall we saw Mackey in *Oriental America* for the Black Patti Troubadours before she took part in *Sons of Ham*.[230-231]

Russell also enjoyed that "March Craig, the contortionist, is indeed a wonder and he is the most natural human, rubber-necked man that ever breathed." [232]

Some of the songs in the show included; 'Dahomian Queen' by Anna Cook, Morris Smith, and Company, 'Swing Along, Mellie Green' by Henry Troy and chorus, 'Broadway in Dahomey' by Williams, Walker, and Company, 'A Rich Coon Man' by Aida Overton Walker, 'Brown Skin Baby of Mine' by Abbie Mitchell and Richard Connors, and 'Leaders of Coloured Aristocracy' by Hattie McIntosh. It also recycled two songs from the previous show: 'My Castle on the River Nile' by Walker and 'Society' previously by Aida Overton but now by Pete Hampton, Hattie McIntosh, Lloyd Gibbs, and Richard Connors.

A significant feature was 'Jonah Man' by Bert Williams. This role established the main pattern for Williams in his following stage performances, that is, a slow unlucky man. Williams explained in 1917, "[e]ven if it rained soup," his character "would be found with a fork in his hand and no spoon in sight." The song was recorded as 'I'm a Jonah Man' by Pete Hampton and Laura Bowman in Europe. They recorded quite a lot, in fact, with more than 80 titles, also listing 'The Mouth Organ Coon,' 'Bill Bailey, Won't You Please Come Home?,' 'Down In Georgia On Camp Meeting Day,' and James Bland's Cakewalk favorite 'Dem Golden Slippers.'

Finally, 'Emancipation Day' by Wiliams and Walker was probably inspired by marches for Emancipation Day which Cook had seen in Washington. Some criticism came from the fact that in the show, the Cakewalk was done hand in hand, like a barn dance, linking the dance to square dancing once again.[233-235]

Williams and Walker were just some of those producing influential shows at the turn of the century. Bob Cole was a new producer, actor, and writer. Cole was born in Athens, Georgia, in 1868. His parents were square dancers, and all the family members knew a musical instrument. After playing in a string quartet in Florida and singing in New Jersey, he toured various Chicago clubs singing, telling jokes, and playing guitar before moving to New York. There, he worked for *The Creole Show*, where he gained some fame and met his future wife, Stella Wiley. In 1894, he formed the All-Star Stock Company, which allowed him to train actors. He performed his song 'The Four Hundred Ball' with his wife for the Black Patti Troubadours.

Due to tensions with the Troubadours, Cole quit the troupe with Billy Johnson, Will Accoe, and a few others, a group for which he wrote the music and lyrics for a brand new show: *A Trip to Coontown*. This parody of *A Trip to Chinatown* was co-produced with veteran Tom Brown and cast Sam Lucas as old man Silas

Green. Willie Wayside, Jesse Shipp, Lloyd Gibbs, and Walter Dixon were other show members. As a result of the animosity with the powerful Troubadours, the show had trouble finding theaters to perform in. It was only through a trip to Canada that it gained momentum before coming back triumphantly to the United States. William Foster was in charge of the publicity, a job he later did for the Williams and Walker team. During their passage in Memphis in 1901, the show was described as "free of vulgarity." The impact of Sam Lucas' song 'I Can Stand for Your Color, but Your Hair Won't Do' was demonstrated by the popularity of ironed hair in the city in the following days. Despite its great success, various lawsuits forced the show to close in 1900.[236-238]

Still competitive, apart from the operatic sections and the Cakewalk contest as previously seen, the Black Patti Troubadours also offered various shows during the same years. *Ragtime Frolic at Rasbury Park* (1900) had Al Watts replacing Ernest Hogan, and his wife Cecil Watts joined him. Also performing were the dancing combination of Ida Forsyne and Grayson, Leslie Triplett, James Lightfoot (who also worked with Williams and Walker), Judson Hicks, May Lange, and Mattie Phillips. Worth mentioning, James Wilson balanced lamps and other delicate objects on himself. A description of the troupe in 1903 mentioned Murriel Ringgold, the "buck dancing wonder," and Clementine Pratt doing The Essence of Old Virginny.[239-240]

Darktown Circus Day (1903) had a book written by Bob Cole before he left Black Patti, with main performers James Crosby, Ida Forsyne, Ed Green, Bobby Kemp, and Leslie Triplett. The chorus line was the Belles of Darktown with Bessie Gillam, Nettie Lewis, Jeanetta Murphy, Olivette Williams, Sarah Green, Emma Thompson, Lizzie Taylor, Maude Turner, Henrietta Percaud, Mable Turner, and Ella Carr. From this lineup, Sarah Green had been in *Rufus Rastus* as part of the Four Creole Belles, Emma Thompson was also a 'coon shouter,' and Lizzie Taylor was in Gideon's Minstrels in 1902, collaborating with juggler and gun manipulator John Pamplin. Taylor was seen as late as 1914 as a comedienne at Devon and Johnson's Café in New York City. The show also included candy butchers, peanut vendors, animal attendants, freaks, monkeys, bears, elephants, and Mack Allen, the slack wire artist.[241-243]

The story happened in a circus tent, outside the tent, and at a theater. The main song and dance acts were 'Strolling around the Circus Tent' by the entire company and 'Mandy' by Ida Forsyne and the chorus. Forsyne also "sang and danced 'Maid of Timbuktu' quite as fascinatingly as ever." [244]

Nettie Lewis, later active in Chicago's Pekin Theater, and Bobby Kemp performed 'Under the Bamboo Tree.' The finale of the show's first half was a buck-and-wing contest. The second part offered Bobby Kemp's Wang Doodle Four, Mack Allen, and operatic selections like 'Waltz Song (Belle of New York).' There was also James Crosby dressed as a giant chicken singing 'Give a Chicken One More Chance.' [245]

Born in Galveston, Texas, in 1867, Kemp started with the team of Moore and Kemp. He worked in the Richard and Pringle circus with Ed Green and John

Rucker in 1899, in which "McCarver, Reed, and McCarver showed themselves capital dancers and acrobats." In 1900, he took part in the Nashville Students as a one-man band. As a comedian and singer, he was in the Black Patti Troubadours with the Wangdoodle Four and sang 'That's the Way to Spell Chicken.' He also had the famous 'Ragtime Millionaire' in his repertoire. His Kemp Comedy Four included Tom Logan.[246-250]

Strangely, the song 'Castle on the Nile' from the Williams and Walker's shows *Sons of Ham* and *In Dahomey* was also sung by James Crosby and company in *Darktown Circus Day*. Crosby was later in the Dandy Dixie Minstrel as an "eccentric dancing comedian" in addition the Tony Trio, "the greatest living acrobatic team." [251]

With this panoply of shows and performers, the table was set for years to come. A myriad of traveling shows offered opportunities to the ever-increasing number of performers eager to make a career in entertainment. Artists like Billy Kersands, Billy McClain, Sam Lucas, the Hyers Sisters, Johnson and Dean, The Brittons, Bob Cole, and Williams and Walker proved it was possible to sustain a long and significant career in the field, and, even more critical, to be successful in building serious productions and touring companies. Members of these troupes, alongside an emerging generation slowly making a name for itself, would define the music, the dance, and the industry for the following decades.

Dances like Juba, buck-and-wing, the Cakewalk, or European-based quadrilles, waltzes, cotillions and the like, evolved in various contexts; rural, urban, and the performing stage. This allowed movements to be copied, changed, parodied, adapted, or invented in various circumstances by a wide range of performers who jumped between companies, troupes, and productions, creating a dense network of interconnected professionals, a well-established and self-aware African American performing cultural group.

1- Cake walkers   2- Cake walkers

1- James Bland   2- Cover of 'Dancing on the Kitchen Floor' (Bland)

Edward Windsor Kemble, 'The Cake-Walk,' (1903)

WM MᶜLAIN

Cake walkers and ragtime sheet music's covers

Previous page: Billy McClain

1- 'Walking for the Cake,' (1889)   2- William Ludlow Sheppard, 'Holiday Games at Richmond, Va.-The Cake Walk. (1870

1- Dandy Jack's Partner 2- The waltz 3 and 4- The Cakewalk

William Dorsey Swann

1- Black Patti   2- Hogan with the Black Patti Troubadours   3- Buck dancing for the Black Patti Troubadours

1- The Black Patti Troubadours with Ernest Hogan   2- Plantation Show

Ida Forsyne

1- Sadie and Joe Britton   2- Frank Mallory in *The Policy Player*   3- The Mallory Brothers with Brooks and Halliday   4- The Mallory Brothers with Maze Brooks and the Hypnotized Chicken act

Following page 1-Mallory Brothers   2- Bohee Brothers

1- Seth Weeks in a quartet   2- Seth Weeks quartet and the Cakewalk

1- The Cakewalk   2- *Oriental America*   3- *Oriental America*   4-Harry Fiddler (1907)

1-Hampton and Johnson in *Darkest America* 2-The Cakewalk in *Darkest America* 3-Walking for Dat Cake   4- Dean and Johnson with cakewalkers   5- Dora Dean

Dean and Johnson

Charles Johnson and Dora Dean

A real six inch punch Je
Dean discovered in the
How beautifully, elegent
would blend with entranc
hence the key note to
years of phenominal suc

Dean and Johnson

Dean and Johnson
Next Page: Dora Dean

Dean and Johnson

1 and 2- Madame Selika   3- Walker and May 4- Ida May

The Four Black Diamonds

1-Orpheus McAdoo's Georgia_Minstrelsn (1900) 2- Cake walkers

1- Cake walker   2-Ed Green   3-Al and Grundy   4-James Grundy   5- Will Marion Cook

1-Cakewalk in Edison's film   2-Cakewalk in *Uncle Tom's Cabin.* (1903)

1-Square dance in Uncle Tom's Cabin   2- Buck dance and Cakewalk in *Uncle Tom's Cabin*   3
and 4- Belle Davis and Pickaninnies

Belle Davis and young dancer

1-3-Belle Davis and Pickaninnies   2-Belle Davis   3-Abbie Mitchell

JENNIE SCHEPER

With best wishes to
my many admirers
Alhambra theatre
Dec. 1910
Paris.

1- Bert Grant, Sadie Jones, and Irving Jones   2- Payton and Harris, Grotesque Cakewalkers   3-
Miss Sheppart   4- M.. and Mrs William Farrell,champion cakewalkers (1898)   5- *In Dahomey*

1- Bob Cole 2- Bert Williams 3- GeorgeWalker 4- Aida Overton and George Walker 5- Aida Overton Walker

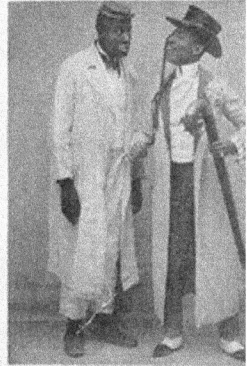

Williams and Walker

From *In Dahomey*; Rhoda King, Jessie Ellis, Birdie Williams and Ida Gigas

1- Scene from *In Dahomey*   2- Williams and Walker's troupe

1- Williams and Walker on 'Jonah Man' (1903)   2- Pete Hampton and Laura Bowman
3- Williams, Overton and Walker in In Dahomey

1- Leslie Triplet   2- Bobby Kemp   3- Cakewalk

1- Muriel Ringgold   2-Bobby Kemp   3- John Rucker   4- Nettie Lewis in *Darktown Circus Day*

HINES and Mdlle. SELLYNA with LITTLE ARTHUR.

1- Cake walkers   2- Hines, Sellyna and Little Arthur   3- Amy Height, singer and dancer

1- Cakewalkers 2- The Hills, Wesley and Ida, in *Darktown Circus Day* 2- Cake walkers

Images are a courtesy of the Library of Congress, the New York Public Library, the Schomburg Center, the Helen Armstead-Johnson Photograph Collection, the Emory archives, Yale University, newspapers, private collections

Notes

1. Blesh, p. 96
2. Abrahams, p. 101
3. Hill, p. 33
4. Haskins, p. 11 and Southern, *Black Music*, p. 253
5. Fletcher, p. 19
6. Abrahams, p. 97
7. Jasen, p. 7
8. Jasen, p. 13
9. Stearns, p. 117
10. Fletcher, p. 91
11. Sampson, *Blacks in Blackface*, p. 298
12. Fletcher, p. xix
13. Sampson, *Blacks in Blackface*, p. 298
14. Abbott and Seroff, *Out of Sight: The Rise of African-American Popular Music:1889-1895,* p. 363
15. Cherry, Kittredge (April 12, 2022). "William Dorsey Swann: Ex-slave fought for queer freedom in 1880s as America's first drag queen". *qspirit.net*. Archived from the original on August 3, 2022. Retrieved April 27, 2022.
16. *The Wichita Star*, January 2, 1889
17. *South Bend Tribune*, July 29, 1889
18. *Lancaster Daily Intelligencer*, September 17, 1888
19. *Owingsville Outlook*, April 16, 1896
20. *The Wilmington Morning Star,* December 3, 1892
21. The Baltimore Sun, October 21, 1885
22. *Evansville Courier*, September 24, 1889
23. *Times Union*, February 28, 1889
24. *Hartford Courant*, October 30, 1889
25. *The Indenpendance Kansan*, April 27, 1881
26. *The Brooklyn Citizen*, December 1926, 1889
27. *Philadelphia Inquirer*, March 30, 1895
28. *Brooklyn Citizen*, March 20, 1891
29. *Buffalo Weekly Express*, February 18, 1892
30. *The Standard Union*, 1895
31. *Brooklyn Citizen*, February 12, 1896
32. *Standard Union*, November 12, 1891
33. The Wichita Eagle, September 12, 1900
34. *The Daily Mail*, February 19, 1894
35. *The Courrier Journal,* March 19, 1892
36. *The Tribune*, June 6, 1889
37. Stearns, p. 71 and Abbott, *Out of Sight,* p. 56
38. Abbott, *Out of Sight,* p. 56
39. Forbes, p. 68
40. Hill, p. 34 and Waldon, p. 25
41. Fletcher, p. 105
42. Ibid, p. 105
43. Ibid p. 107
44. Ibid, p. 107
45. Ibid, p. 107
46. Ibid, p. 125
47. Stearns, p. 123, from Fletcher
48. Fletcher,p. 103 and Abbott, *Out of Sight,* p. 157
49. Abbott, *Out of Sight*, p. 157
50. Lee, p. 33-35
51. Bogle, p. 24
52. As noticed by Abbott and Seroff
53. Lee, p. 102

54. Ibid, p. 97
55. Ibid, p. 98
56. Ibid,p. 102
57. Ibid, p. 117 and Carter, p. 49
58. Lee, p. 119
59. Ibid, p. 124
60. Ibid, p. 131
61. Abbott and Seroff, *Ragged but Right,* p. 40
62. Sampson, *Blacks in Blackface,* p. 219
63. Abbott and Seroff, *Out of Sight,* p. 363
64. Sampson, *Blacks in Blackface,* p. 228
65. Hill, p. 34
66. Stearns, p. 251
67. Ibid, p. 251
68. Music City Center Interview
69. Stearns, p. 250
70. Music City Center Interview
71. Sampson, Blacks in Blackface, p. 2268
72. Music City Center Interview
73. Stearns, p. 251 and Sampson, Blacks in Blackface, p. 2268
74. Fletcher, p. 177
75. Egan, p. 4
76. Stearns, p. 122
77. Steans, p. 289
78. Sampson, *Blacks in Blackface,* p. 25
79. Abbott and Seroff, *Ouit of Sight,* p. 154-155
80. Wynn, p. 76-77
81. *Black Europe.* Bear Family record, Cd Box Set, 2013
82. Abbott and Seroff, *Out of Sight,* p. 160
83. Ibid, p. 161
84. Ibid, p. 161
85. Ibid, p. 163
86. Ibid, p. 163
87. Ibid,, p. 163
88. *Battle Creek Enquirer,* December 23, 1951
89. Abbott and Seroff, *Out of Sight,* p. 163
90. Ibid, p. 164
91. Ibid, p. 164
92. Sampson, *Blacks In Blackface,* p. 26 and *Boston Globe,* May 8, 1900
93. Abbott and Seroff, *Out of Sight,* p. 164 and Sampson, *Blacks in Blackface,* p. 25
94. Sampson, Blacks in Blackface, p. 241
95. Ibid, p. 611 and *The Daily Item,* February 23, 1910
96. *Boston Globe,* Oct 9, 1904
97. *Newark Stark Eagle,* 1910
98. *The Courrier,* May 2 1909
99. *New York Age,* June 10, 1909
100. *The Dayton Herald,* October , 1908
101. *Buffalo Courrier,* May 25, 1909
102. *New York Age,* October 29, 1908
103. *New York Age,* September 23, 1909
104. Stearns, p. 118
105. Abbott and Seroff, *Out of Sight,* p. 167
106. Ibid, p. 166
107. Ibid, p. 166 and 220
108. Ibid, p. 167
109. Stearns, p. 118
110. Pepener, p. 32 and Sampson, *Blacks in Blackface,* p. 27
111. Sampson, *Blacks in Blackface,* p. 101
112. Morgan, p. 38
113. Sampson, *Blacks in Blackface,* p. 100
114. J.W. Johnson, p. 97
115. Toll, p. 263
116. Fletcher, p. 94 and Abbott and Seroff, *Out of Sight,* p. 380 and 333
117. Abbott, *Out of Sight,* p. 391

118. Ibid, p. 380
119. Ibid, 333 and New York Clipper
120. Abbott and Seroff, *Out of Sight,* p. 234
121. Sampson, *Blacks in Blackface*, p. 22
122. Dawson, p. 2
123. Abbott and Seroff, *Out of Sight*, p. 484
124. Ibid, p. 443 and *They All Played Ragtime*, p. 71
125. Floyd, p. 70
126. Pugh p. 100
127. Southern, *Images*, p. 239
128. Bogle, *Bright Boulevards, Bold Dreams: The Story of Black Hollywood*, p. 11-12
129. Sampson, *Blacks in Blackface*, p. 1842
130. Fletcher, p. 108-109
131. Stearns, p. 287
132. Haskins, *Black Dance in America: A History Through its People,* p. 28
133. Letter to Handy, reprinted in Handy, p.39
134. Fletcher, p. 109
135. On the LP, *Reunion in Ragtime,*
136. Stearns, p. 286
137. Fletcher, p. 109
138. Stearns, p. 266
139. Haskins, *Mr. Bojangles*, p. 238
140. Fletcher, p. 41
141. *Battle Creek Enquirer*, December 23, 1951
142. Fletcher, p. 112
143. Sampson, *Blacks in Blackface*, p. 495
144. Fletcher, p. 112
145. Sampson, *Blacks in Blackface*, p. 113
146. The Four Black Diamonds (ca. 1905-1922) – Black Central Europe
147. Graham, p. 183
148. Ibid, p. 196
149. Abbott and Seroff, *Out of Sight*, p. 250
150. Graham, p. 206
151. Abbott and Seroff, *Out of Sight,* p. 127
152. Ibid, p. 127
153. Ibid, p. 129
154. Ibid, p. 132
155. Fletcher, p. 141
156. Abbott and Seroff, *Out of Sight*, p. 132
157. Abbott and Seroff, *Out of Sight*, p. 132 and p. 134
158. Ibid, p. 135-137
159. Ibid, p. 138
160. Graham, p. 218
161. Abbott and Seroff, *Out of Sight*, p. 363, 368 and 373 and Sampson, *Blacks in Blackface*, p. 2228
162. *Philadelphia Inquirer*, June 1, 1900
163. *Washington Times*, April 19, 1898
164. *Pittsburgh Daily Post*, April 10, 1898
165. Sampson, *Blacks in Blackface*, p. 244
166. Hill, p. 28
167. Sampson, *Blacks in Blackface*, p. 221
168. Carter, p. 8-12
169. Lee, p. 53
170. Jasen, p. 84
171. Carter, p. 38-39
172. Brooke Baldwin (1981). 'The Cakewalk: Study in Stereotype and Reality.' *Journal of Social History*. **15** (2): 205–18.
173. Jasen, p. 85
174. Carter, p. 47-48
175. Johnson, p. 103
176. Carter, p. 53-54
177. *The Evening News*, June 29, 1899
178. *Evening Express*, September 27, 1900
179. *Boston Globe*, December 16, 1900
180. *Chicago Tribune*, March 3. 1901
181. *Boston Post*, May 27, 1902

182. *The Boston Globe*, December 28, 1902
183. *Pittsburg Press*, March 8, 1903
184. *Topeka Plainleader*, April 23, 1909
185. Sampson, *Blacks in Blackface*, p. 334
186. Sampson, *Blacks in Blackface*, p. 473 and 1167
187. Abbott and Seroff, *The Original Blues*, p. 9 and 16
188. *Wilkes-Barre Time Reader*, December 16, 1902
189. *Greenfield Daily Recorder*, January 28, 1905
190. *The North Adams Transcript*, January 31, 1903
191. *Austin American Statesman*, June 21, 1901
192. Sampson, *Blacks in Blackface*, p. 212
193. Abbott and Seroff, *The Original Blues*, p. 216
194. Sampson, *Blacks in Blackface*, p. 1852
195. Abbott and Seroff, *Ragged but Right*, p. 23-24
196. Sampson, *Blacks in Blackface*, p. 1737
197. Abbott and Seroff, *The Original Blues,* p. 33
198. Forbes, p. 30
199. Abbott and Seroff, *Out of Sight*, p. 289
200. Handy, p. 39
201. Stearns, p. 86
202. Forbes, p. 65
203. Stearns, p. 122
204. Stearns, p. 122
205. Cooper, p. 135
206. Hill, p. 35
207. Sampson, *Blacks in Blackface*, p. 191
208. J.W. Johnson, p. 104-105
209. Sampson, *Blacks in Blackface*, p. 2293
210. Jasen, p. 44
211. Carter, p. 38-39
212. Ibid, p. 45
213. Sampson, *Blacks and Blackface*, p. 2354
214. Ibid, p. 119
215. Music City Center Interview
216. Carter, p. 46
217. Sampson, *Blacks in Blackface*, p. 2277
218. Ibid, p. 1759
219. Abbott and Seroff, Ragged But Right, p. 59
220. Sampson, *Blacks in Blackface*, p. 2352
221. Ibid, p. 281
222. Ibid, p. 1172
223. Ibid, p. 2309
224. Ibid, p. 2311
225. Lane, p. 40
226. Carter, p. 56
227. Forbes p. 107
228. Music City Center Interview
229. Carter, p. 57
230. Sampson, *Black in Blackface*, p. 1178
231. Ibid, p. 1178
232. Ibid, p. 1178
233. Ibid,p. 1376
234. Carter, p. 62
235. Carter, p. 66
236. Lane, p. 27, and Sampson, *Blacks in Blackface*, p. 2300
237. Sampson, *Blacks in Black and White: A Source Book on Black Films*, p. 172
238. Sampson, *Blacks in Blackface*, p. 1174
239. Ibid, p. 1186
240. *The Rison Son*, February 6, 1903
241. Sampson, *Blacks in Blackface*, p. 1853
242. Ibid, p. 1048
243. Ibid, p. 1567
244. *Ashbury Park Morning Press*, July 29, 1904
245. Sampson, *Blacks in Blackface,,* p. 1191

246. Ibid, p. 1736 and 1810
247. Ibid, p. 1818
248. Abbott and Seroff, *Ragged But Right,* p. 28
249. Ibid, p. 33
250. Sampson, *Blacks in Blackface*, p. 228
251. Ibid, p. 1873

Glossary

Chorus: Group of singers and dancers performing as a group or to back a lead performer for a song

Coon song: Ragtime song in which the lyrics portray a caricatural, often negative, image of African Americans. They were popular mostly in the 1890s and 1900s

Olio: Middle part of a minstrel shows, usually dedicated to novelty numbers

Pickaninny: African American child performer in the trend of racial caricatures

Soubrette: One of the leading female performer in a show

Bibliography

Abbott, Lynn and Doug Seroff. *Out of Sight: The Rise of African-American Popular Music:1889-1895*. University Press of Mississippi. 2002

Abbott and Seroff. *Ragged but Right; Black Traveling Shows, Coon Songs and the Black Pathway to Blues and Jazz*. University Press of Mississippi. 2009

Abbott, Lynn and Doug Seroff. *The Original Blues: The Emergence of the Blues in African-American Vaudeville*. University Press of Mississippi, 2017.

Abrahams, Roger D.. *Singing the Master: The Emergence of African-American Culture in the Plantation South*. Penguin Books, 1992.

Absher, Amy. *The Black Musician and the City: Race and Music in Chicago, 1900-1967*. University of Michigan Press, 2014.

Alger, Dean. 2014. *The Original Guitar Hero and The Power of Music: The Legendary Lonnie Johnson, Music and Civil Rights*. University of North Texas Press

Allen, William Francis, Charles Pickard Ware, and Lucy McKim Garrison. *Slave Songs of the United States*. A. Simpson & Co., 1867

Allen, James, Hilton Als, Congressman John Lewis and Leon F. Litwack. *Whitout Sanctuary: Lynching Photography in America*. Twin Palms Publishers, 2010.

Barlow, William. *Looking Up at Down: The Emergence of Blues Culture*. Temple University Press. 1989

Blesh, Rudi. *Shining Trumpets: A History of Jazz*. Knopf, 1946

Bogle, Donald. *Bright Boulevards, Bold Dreams: The Story of Black Hollywood*. Ballantine Books, 2005

Bogle, Donald. *Toms, Coons, Mulattoes, Mamies & Bucks: An Interpretive History of Blacks in American Films*. Continuum, 1996

Bradford, Perry. *Born With the Blues: Perry Bradford's Own Story*. Oak Publications, 1965

Broonzy, William Lee Conley and Yannick Bruynoghe. *Big Bill Blues*. Lndd, (1956), 1977

Brown Douglas, Kelly. *Black Bodies and the Black Church: A Blues Slant*. Pelgrave MacMillan, 2012

Buerkle, Jack V. and Danny Barker. *Bourbon Street Black: The New Orleans Black Jazzman*. Oxford University Press, 1973

Carter, Marva Griffin. *Swing Along:The Musical Life of Will Marion Cook*. Oxford University Press, 2008

Charters, Samuel. *Songs of Sorrow: Lucy McKim Garrison and Slave Songs of the United States*. University Press of Mississippi. 2015

Cone, James H. *The Spirituals and the Blues*. Orbis Books. 2012

Curtis, Susan. *Dancing to a Black Man's Tune: A Life of Scott Joplin*. University of Missouri Press. 1994

Dawson, Jim. *The Twist: The Story of the Song and Dance that Changed the World*. Faber & Faber, 1995.

DeFrantz, Thomas F.. *Dancing Many Drums : Excavations ions in African-American Dance*. The University of Wisconsin Press, 2002

Dixon Gottschild, Brenda. *Digging the Africanist Presence In American Performance: Dance and Other Contexts*. Greenwood Press, 1996

Douglas-Chin, Richard J., 2001. *Preacher Woman Sings the Blues : The Autobiographies of Nineteeth-Century African American Evangelists*. University Press of Missouri. 2001

Douglas, Kelly Brown. Black *Bodies and the Black Church: A Blus Slant*. Palgrave MacMillan. 2012

Du Bois, W.E.B., 1903. *The Souls of Black Folk*. Dover Publications

Dyonne Thompson, Katrina. *Ring Shout, Wheel About: The Racial Politics of Music and Dance in North American Slavery*. University of Illinois Press, 2014

Egan,Bill. *Florence Mills: Harlem Jazz Queen*. Scarecrow Press, 2004

Emery, Lynne Fauley. *Black Dance from 1619 to Today*. Second Edition. Dance Horizons Book. Princeton Book Company 1988

Epstein, Dena. *Sinful Tunes and Spirituals; Black Folk Music to the Civil War*. University of Illinois Press. 2003

Fletcher, Tom. *The Tom Fletcher Story: 100 Years of the Negro in Show Business*. Burdge & Company, 1954

Floyd, Samuel A.. *The Power of Black Music: Interpreting Its History From Africa to the United States*. Oxford University Press, 1999.

Floyd, Samuel A., with Melanie L. Zeca and Guthrie P. Ramsey Jr. *The Transformation of Black Music.: The Rhythm, the Songs, and the Ships of the African Diaspora*. Oxford University Press, 2017

Forbes, Camille, F., *Introducing Berth Williams: Burnt Cork, Broadway, and the Story of America's First Black Star.* Basic Civitas Books, 2008

Gaunt, Kyra D.. *The Games Black Girls Play: Learning the Ropes from Double Dutch to Hip-Hop*. New York University Press. 2006

Giola, Ted. *History of Jazz*. Oxford University Press, 1997

Goffin, Robert. *La Nouvelle-Orléans, capitale du jazz*. Éditions de la Maison Française. 1946

Graham, Sandra Jean. *Spirituals and the Birth of a Black Entertainment Industry*. University of Illinois Press, 2018

Guarino, Lindsay and Wendy Oliver Ed. *Jazz Dance: A History of the Roots and Branches*. University Press of Florida, 2014

Hammond, Brian, Patrick O'Connor and Elizabeth Welch. *Josephine Baker*. Bulfinch Press, 1988

Handy, W.C., *Father of the Blues*. Collier Books, (1941) 1970

Haskins, James. *Black Dance in America: A History Through its People*.Thomas Y. Crowell, 1990

Hazzard-Gordon, Katrina, *Jookin': The Rise of Social Dance Formations in African-American Culture*. Temple University Press. 1990

Hersch, Charles. *Subversive Sounds; Race and the Birth of Jazz in New Orleans*. The University of Chicago Press. 2007

Herzhaft, Gérard. *Americana; Histoire des musiques de l'Amérique du Nord*. Librairie Arthème Fayard. 2005

Hill, Constance Valis. *Tap Dancing America: A Cultural History*. Oxford University Press, 2010

Hurston, Zora Neale. *The Sanctified Church*. Turtle Island, 1981

Jason, David A. and Gene Jones. *Black Bottom Stomp: Eight Masters of Ragtime and Early Jazz*. Routledge, 2002

Jason, David A. and Trebor Jay Tichenor. *Rags and Ragtime; A Musical Journey.* Continuum Book, 1978

Jasen, David A. and Gene Jones. *Spreadin' Rhythm Around: Black Popular Songwriters, 1880-1930.* Schirmer Books, 1998

Johnson,James Weldon, *Black Manhattan.*(1930) 1958

Johnson Reagon, Bernice. *We'll Understand it Better By and By: Pioneering African American Gospel Composers.* Smithsonian Institution Press, 1992

Jones, William P., *The Tribe of Black Ulysses: African American Lumber Workers in the Jim Crow South.* University of Illinois Press, 2005

Kmen, Henry. *Music in New Orleans: The Formative Years 1791-1841.* Louisiana State University Press, 1966

Kubik, Gerhard. *Africa and the Blues.* University Press of Mississippi. 1999

Lane. Stewart F. *Black Broadway: African Americans on the Great White Way.* SquareOne Publishers, 2015

Lee, Maureen D.. *Sissirietta Jones: "The Greatest Singer of Her Race" 1868-1933.* The University of South Carolina Press, 2012

Lekis, Lisa. *Dancing Gods.* The Scarecrow Press, 1960

Lhamon Jr, William T., *Raising Cain: Représentations du blackface de Jim Crow à Michael Jackson.* Traduit de l'anglais par Sophie Renaut. Kargot & L'Éclat, 2004, President and Fellows of Harvard College, 1998

Long, Richard A.. *The Black Tradition in American Dance.* Photographs selected and annotated by Joe Nash. Prion, 1989

Malnig, Julie, Editor. *Ballroom, Boogie, Shimmy Sham, Shake: A Social and Popular Dance Reader.* University of Illinois Press. 2009

Malone, Jacqui. *Steppin' on the Blues; the Visible Rhythms of African American Dances.* University of Illinois Press. 1995

McCuster, John. *Creole Trombone: Kid Ory and the Early Years of Jazz.* University Press of Mississippi, 2012

Morgan, Thomas L. and William Barlow. *From Cakewalk to Concert Halls: An Illustrated History of African American Popular Music from 1895 to 1930.* Elliott & Clark Publishing, 1992

Odum, Howard W. and Guy B. Johnson. 1926. *Negro Workaday Songs.* University of North Carolina Press. 1926

Oliver, Paul. *Songsters and Saints; Vocal Traditions on Race Records.* 1984

Pepener III, John O. *African-American Concert Dance: The Harlem Renaissance and Beyond.* University of Illinois Press, 2001

Peterson, B.L., Bernard. *Profiles of African American Stage Performers and Theater People: 1816-1960.* Greenwood press, 2001

Pugh, Megan. *America Dancing: From the Cakewalk to the Moonwalk.* Yale University Press, 2015

Riis, Thomas L. *Just Before Jazz: Black Musical Theater in New York, 1890 to 1915.* Smithsonian Institution Press, 1989

Rosenbaum, Art and Margo Newmark Rosenbaum. *Shout Because You're Free: The African American Ring Shout Tradition in Coastal Georgia.* The University of Georgia Press, 1998

Sammond, Nicholas. *Birth of an Industry: Blackface Minstrelsy and the Rise of American Animation.* Duke University Press, 2015

Sampson, Henry T. *Blacks in Blackface: A Source Book on Early Black Musical Shows.* Scarecrow Press. Numerical version. 2014

Smith, Christopher J. *The Creolization of American Culture: William Sidney Mount and the Roots of Blackface Minstrelsy.* University of Illinois Press, 2013

Smith, Willie "the Lion", and George Hoefer. *Music On My Mind: The Memoirs of an American Pianist.* Da Capo Press, 1964

Southern, Eileen. *The Music of Black Americans: A History.* Second Edition. W. W. Norton & Company. 1983

Southern, Eileen and Josephine Wright. *Images: Iconography of Music In African-American Culture, 1770s-1920s.* Garland Publishing, Inc., 2000

Stearns, Marshall and Jean. *Jazz Dance: The Story of American Vernacular Dance.* Da Capo Press. (1968) 1994

Talley, Thomas W. Compiler. *Negro Folk Rhymes: Wise and Otherwise, With a Study.* Forgotten Books (1922) 2012

Toll, Robert C., *Blacking Up: The Mionstrel Show in Nineteenth-Century America.* Oxford University Press, 1974

Tucker, Linda G., *Lockstep and Dance : Images of Black Men in Popular Culture.* University Press of Mississippi, 2007

Valis Hill, Constance. *Tap Dancing America : A Cultural History.* Oxford University Press, 2010

Waldo, Terry. *This is Ragtime.* Foreword by Eubie Blake. Da Capo Press, 1971, 1991

White, Shane and Graham White. *Sound of Slavery: Discovering African American History Through Songs, Sermons, and Speech.* Beacon Press. 2005

Wondrich, David, *Stomp and Swerve: American Music Gets Hot 1843-1924.* Chicago Review Press. 2003

Wood, Marcus. *Blind Memory: Visual Representations of Slavery in England and America 1780-1865.* Routledge, 2000

Wynn, Neil A. Editor. *Cross the Water Blues: African American Music in Europe.* University Press of Mississippi. 2007

www.ingramcontent.com/pod-product-compliance
Lightning Source LLC
Chambersburg PA
CBHW061828040426
42447CB00012B/2871